FUNNY
PECULIAR

FUNNY PECULIAR

THE AUTOBIOGRAPHY

Will Young

With illustrations by
Kathryn Pinker

SPHERE

First published in Great Britain in 2012 by Sphere
Reprinted 2012 (twice)

A CIP catalogue record for this book
is available from the British Library.

ISBN HB 978-0-7515-5011-5
ISBN CF 978-0-7515-5012-2

Typeset in Bembo by M Rules
Printed and bound in Great Britain by
Clays Ltd, St Ives plc

Papers used by Sphere are from well-managed forests
and other responsible sources.

MIX
Paper from
responsible sources
FSC
www.fsc.org FSC® C104740

Sphere
An imprint of
Little, Brown Book Group
100 Victoria Embankment
London EC4Y 0DY

An Hachette UK Company
www.hachette.co.uk

www.littlebrown.co.uk

For my family
and friends

Contents

'He also gets depression...'

'...and introducing Will Young. He famously battled Simon Cowell ten years ago and went on to win *Pop Idol*. It hasn't all been plain sailing, though – he also gets depression, and he's here to sing his hit single, "Jealousy"!'

The lights fade up.

I am singing on a late-night show in Dublin.

Really, I'm thinking. *That* is my introduction? I mean, I've had a few in my time but I think this could be the winner: 'He's here to sing for you, but guess what... he gets depressed! He might even be depressed *at this very moment*! We just don't know and, people, listen to the lyrics of the song... JEALOUSY! He must get *very* depressed to write these songs! Anyway, enjoy this one, it's upbeat but the lyrical content is actually very depressing.'

I am laughing inside, though. And luckily this is a rehearsal, so as I am singing the song, trying to catch various camera angles while perving on the mime band that's been hired for the evening, I decide I will ask if we can change the introduction. Either that or we could just start the performance by swinging the cameras round to reveal me hanging from a noose.

'He gets depression... look, it got the better of him. The back catalogue is out now.'

Faye, my day-to-day manager, comes up to me after the sound check.

'We've changed the introduction.'

'Oh, great.'

'Yes, we've changed it to: "Here is Will Young, who gets depression and is also on meths." Thought that would be better.'

'Much better. Thank you, Faye.'

Faye smiles. 'Pleasure.'

The truth is that I do get depression. I suffer from extremely low self-esteem and a lack of confidence. In technical jargon, I carry shame, I am co-dependent, I suffer from love addiction and depression . . . In other words I am a psychotherapist's smorgasbord!

It's bizarre, because in one area of my life – my work – I am as strong as an ox. And yet in another I can sometimes be as weak as a feather in the wind. I stress 'sometimes' because it is getting better and I certainly don't write this for pity. It is just a simple fact. If it wasn't for my singing, I'm not sure I would even be around today. Singing has been the one place where I have found my true, powerful self. The one place where I can express what I am feeling and believe that I am being heard. I feel wise in my singing. I feel wise in my career.

I've had to deal with some tricky things in the ten years since winning *Pop Idol*, but I took them in my stride. Actual, real events, things that just happen in life – I can cope with these hardcore facts. I don't have to question them. I never see them as insurmountable. They're real and I know I will survive. It's what lies inside my head that has been hard to deal with. The inner dialogue of questioning and uncertainty.

The tape that goes round and round, constantly jumping from one argument to another. It's like fighting a shadow, or an enemy who keeps morphing into a new opponent.

Standing on a stage in front of sixty thousand people at the Diana tribute concert, singing a song that is challenging at the best of times while doing a dance routine I have only just learned and negotiating speakers that have been left out by accident – that's a doddle. But standing there while in the back of my mind a voice is saying, 'You are the most useless piece of shit on this stage. No one is interested in this. Your boyfriend is sitting in the audience and he is so much better than you and is probably thinking, "God, this is awful." You look fat. Your dancing is atrocious. This is the beginning of the end for your career' – all of those disgusting thoughts and words come flying at me . . . Now, *they* are much harder to take.

By the time I appeared on *Pop Idol*, I had already been through three years of depression, on and off. I remember standing in front of the judges and actually feeling protected by my experiences of sadness. They enveloped me like a cloak. I had been heartbroken. I had struggled – and would continue to struggle – with my sexuality. I had lost friends and experienced family hardship . . . And I had a degree in Politics to boot!

Anyway, this book isn't a rambling account of my day-to-day sadnesses (as riveting as that would be). It is an account of experiences in my life – both now and from my past. It came about through some happy accidents, and it's been fascinating not only to look back but to discover how much I enjoy expressing myself through writing. Some of the stories are sad, some are hysterical, some are painful and some are just the most wonderful things ever to happen in my life. Like the game Angry Birds on my iPhone. Simply life-changing.

Horrid Hell

This was the pet name of my prep school. Horrid Hell. Its real name was Horris Hill.

I'd grown up knowing all about Horris Hill. Both my uncles had gone to school there (one of them had even been a teacher there for a while), and my grandfather had been a governor – in fact, my grandparents lived just on the edge of the school grounds, and the slate from their old house had been used on the school roof. In the summer months we had the place largely to ourselves – I even learned to swim in the school swimming pool. So Horris Hill was very much woven into my life, and in particular life with my grandparents.

I was seven when I moved there from my previous school with Rupert, my twin brother. It had always been a boarding school but that year they had accepted day boys for the first time. This meant you could arrive in time for chapel in the morning and leave before chapel in the evening. My sister Emma went to school up the road so it was an easy run for my mum. We didn't board at first, largely for financial reasons. My father had just started a new business and the family couldn't afford to pay the fees. As it was, we had a deal with the school due to our family connections – two for the price of one!

I know a lot of people look back on their schooldays with real nostalgia. But I might as well come out and say it – from my point of view, when I was a pupil there, Horris Hill was one of the sickest, most twisted and archaic educational institutions you could imagine. It provided me with many hysterical memories and funny tales of Billy Bunter-type hilarity, but it gave me no nurturing, no love, no warmth and absolutely no preparation for anything pertaining to normal life. Looking back, it seems to me that quite a few of the staff – particularly the men – were emotionally repressed. Men who operated in a bubble. Some of the women were as cold as ice too, though I loved my piano teacher, Miss Wakeley, and the matrons.

Even the teachers' pets were cold and indifferent, providing no joy or love. And when I say pets, I literally mean their dogs – aloof, strange, emotionless animals. They would walk right past us, showing no interest in our attempts to stroke them. I was used to dogs that bounded up and licked you in the face and then charged off after a ball. But these dogs were impeccably behaved to the point of oddness. They stuck close to their masters and were completely indifferent to any of the boys.

Trying to find a drop of love and kindness in this place was for me – a lot of the time – like searching for life-giving water in the desert. I am forever grateful that I had such strong family links with Horris Hill and that I had Rupert with me every step of the way, for if I hadn't the place would have fucked me up for eternity. To be honest it has done a pretty good job of that anyway, contributing to a lot of pain and suffering.

Perhaps some old pupils from that time have other memories and would recount their experiences very differently. However, I'm certainly not the only one to feel as I do about it. I have run into a number of former pupils over the last ten years who have shared similar stories. When I was living in Notting Hill I bumped into a boy a few years younger than me in my local supermarket. (He was quite handsome, actually!) He had nothing but bad words to say about his schooldays. Another time I was at a party at the Serpentine Gallery and met a boy who was in the same year as me. He couldn't even bring himself to speak of his time there, to the point that he crossed the room to get away from me. On another occasion, Rupert and I were doing an interview together on Radio 5 Live about his charity, The Mood Foundation, which he had set up to help people with depression. A man rang in who was very complimentary about Rupert, saying he remembered him at school as a larger-than-life generous character. He then proceeded to tear apart the regime at Horris Hill at the time. The list goes on. A friend of mine is seeing a boy who was a year or so below me. He says the same thing about the school. In all honesty, I have never heard a good word spoken about Horris Hill around the time I was educated there. We had been forced to endure an institution that stifled any free thinking, leaving pupils feeling badly about themselves, with no sense of how to be a happy young boy.

I say 'boy' because, of course, it was a single-sex school. Interaction with girls simply never occurred. I was seventeen before I encountered girls within the education system! At this stage, I could rather neatly imply that if it wasn't for my prep school and my weekly watching of *Dynasty* at my grandparents' house, I would be a full-blooded heterosexual man. In fact, if it wasn't for Alexis Colby's shoulder pads and regular boys' showers, I might be shooting videos with beach babes rather than dancing with male mannequins in Iceland! That could be a whole chapter in itself. But, alas, it's not true. Contrary to what many a priest and radical Christian Scientist might argue, I was always destined to be a lover of men. As my grandmother once elegantly put it, 'Well, you always said you wanted to be a ballet dancer.'

And there you have it.

I can't nail Horris Hill for my sexuality, but I sure as hell can get it for just about everything else.

It was an impressive-looking school. In impressive grounds. Every day, we would turn off the main road coming out of Newbury towards Winchester. I remember sitting in the back of my mum's Escort XR3i with Lenny Kravitz or Terence Trent D'Arby playing on the stereo and feeling the change in the vibrations of the car as we headed off the old A road and on to the smooth, noiseless tarmac of the long school drive that swept down past woods on the left and fields dotted with Shetland ponies on the right. As we levelled out into a mini valley we would pass the junior football pitch (where I once imagined I was Black Beauty) and more fields, overlooked by the school launderette. The drive then curved up and forked, with one branch going to the 'private side' and the headmaster's house and the other leading to the main building. This road opened out into a large car park, surrounded by the swimming pool, four tennis courts and the school sports hall, which also accommodated school concerts and plays. Along from that was the old gym and the squash courts. Beyond the main building was the school chapel and then a common, which was also a six-hole golf course and running track. If you stayed on this road, eventually you would reach the exit through some more woods, passing my grandparents' house along the way.

So you certainly couldn't fault Horris Hill on its facilities. I mean, we had two squash courts and a photo lab! The art school was brand new when I was there and we even had an old printing room.

'Feel that polyester, Margaret'

The printing room was run by Mr Brown. Now Mr Brown, I think, was one of the normal men. He was from Yorkshire, if I remember right. There was something rather endearing about him – he was a gentle-looking man with quite a jowly, open, soft face, and everything he owned seemed to be from the late seventies, from his swimming trunks to his sunglasses to his car. He always wore a pair of baggy brown trousers, a knitted tie and soft black shoes. He ran all of the fun things at Horris Hill: the model train track (which was amazing), the swimming pool and the school shop, as well as the printing room. (The 'shop' wasn't anything special, just a stationery cupboard by his desk, but Mr Brown had *every piece of stationery* you could imagine.) Because of all his jobs, he would walk around with the most enormous set of keys jingling from a chain, attached to his belt loops.

Mr Brown lived with Mrs Brown in a house in the woods just down from the tennis courts. Now Marian Brown was a woman to behold. I'll never forget overhearing her say to my grandmother (who was known by all the teachers), 'Margaret, you know I went to Camp Hopsons to get this scarf. I saw it, I tried it on and really it goes to show . . . you pay for quality, Margaret. Feel that polyester, Margaret, just feel it.'

'How lovely,' my grandmother replied.

Camp Hopsons was the local department store in Newbury and hadn't changed since the 1930s. It did a great range of padded coat hangers and Hoover bags and obviously a very nice scarf. But the way Mrs Brown was talking, it could have been Hermès' flagship store in Paris!

Mrs Brown was a rather stern-looking character, I thought. Her face reminded me of an American eagle's. Her eyes, and the way she moved, were bird-like, too. She had long auburn hair and – like her husband – she was fond of a knit. Nothing was ever floaty. Her summer dresses were made of what looked like curtain material and she always wore a sensible shoe or sandal. She was, in short, terrifying . . . so it was ironic that she had the task of looking after the first years. Every September, at the start of the school year, these poor seven-year-old boys would walk into their new classroom to be confronted with this spindly, bony raptor of a woman, who marched between the desks in her sandals. She would rap your knuckles with a ruler or slap you behind the legs if you did something wrong. Her favourite routine involved teaching the correct way to ask for something. It would go like this:

'Young 1, what do you want?'

(We were all called by our surnames and any brothers were numbered. As I was the oldest by ten minutes, I was Young 1. Rupert was Young 2. Why to God we were called by our surnames I do not know. It was like working in a 1920s bank, aged seven.)

'Young 1. What do you want?'

'Mrs Brown, could I please borrow your pencil sharpener?'

'You COULD borrow my pencil sharpener,' she would reply with relish.

Oh, God, here we go.

'Er . . . Mrs Brown, *may* I borrow your pencil sharpener?'

'You MAY borrow my pencil sharpener.' The 'may' being extended to MAYYYYYYY to allow full emphasis.

'Er . . . *can* I borrow your pencil sharpener?'

'You CAAAAAAAAAAAAAAAN borrow my pencil sharpener.'

'*Will* you let me borrow your pencil sharpener?' (*You silly bitch.*)

'I WILL let you borrow my pencil sharpener, Young 1. Come and get it,' she would proclaim triumphantly, with a tight-lipped smile.

This felt like it happened every bloody lesson. I would

sit there at my desk, running through how the conversation would go before I finally snapped and smacked her in the face. In my imagination, she was tied to her chair at her desk with me and all the other children getting our own back on the old hawk.

'Mrs Brown, may I kick you in the shins?'

'You MAYYYYYY kick me in the shins.'

'Oh, Mrs Brown, could I wee on your feet, please?'

'You COULD wee on my feet.'

'Mrs Brown, would you let...Oh, fuck it.' *KER-POWWW!* And with that, Mrs Brown would be bazookered off this earth. We could all run free and maybe even call each other by our – sin of sins – *first names*. Hooray!

Of course, this never happened and all I ever learned from Mrs Brown was how to ask, in the oddest fashion, for a pencil sharpener.

Another female teacher was Mrs Wainwright-Maxwell. Odd name. Odd lady. She was actually quite pretty and had a softer demeanour than old Marian Brown. Well, at least she may have *appeared* softer, but she was also as cold as ice. Almost more frightening, in a way.

I would often see the teachers interact with each other or with the parents and they would be all sweetness and light, but when they were in the classroom this would change. It was as if they were almost conditioned not to show any love, joy, fun, sensitivity or softness towards the boys.

It's funny, because even as I write this (and I have gone through really good therapy to get all of this shit out) I still feel some anger and sadness. Because all of these memories come from the experiences of my younger self. What I mean is, I must have known and felt their hypocrisy back then. And I did. I remember feeling outraged and perplexed by these odd people who were suddenly in charge of me. I had never seen anything like it. I don't want to write a character assassination of them. That would be pointless. But I do want to show my experience of the school and the people in it. So when I write about these people I write from my truth. They could have been wonderful friends, partners and family members out of school, but for the most part they were – from my perspective – shitty, shitty teachers.

But not Mr Brown. He was an interesting man. And, as he ran many of the things I was interested in, our paths crossed a lot. He was also in charge of everything techy. If there was a problem, Mr Brown would fix it. He could mend a light. He could rescue your frisbee from a tree. He was always doing *something* and if you got in with him and became one of 'Browny's Boys', you were guaranteed some fun jobs.

The printing room stood between the music block and the art department. I never discovered who decided that we should have access to a whopping great printing press, but it was so and it was *fantastic*! With Mr Brown at the helm we learned how to use the different fonts – Times New Roman, Times Bold, etc. – and then how to assemble the individual letters into words, sentences and paragraphs. Each letter was a raised mark at the end of a tiny lead block. You would put them together and hold them firmly in place with blocks of wood. These would then be squeezed by presses on either side. When you had everything in place, you would put it onto the machine, make sure your paper was in position, apply the ink onto the roller and away you went. It was the best fun. There was something extremely satisfying about seeing this huge old printer bursting into life and words appearing on the paper, words that you had painstakingly crafted, letter by leaden letter. I would create headed letter-writing paper for home – in fact, anything that could have a heading did. The smell of the ink, the noise of the printer, cranking away . . . It was brilliant!

As well as making things up for fun, we printed out the

Sunday service sheets every weekend, and bigger jobs such as the programmes for school concerts and plays. I rose up the ranks from junior printer and by the end I was one of the few allowed to be left in charge of the printing room, along with my trusty band of friends – De Halpert, Castoro and Lewis. None of us really played sport (although I wasn't bad at football), so instead we helped Browny with his jobs and basically got into trouble. We would rule the roost in the printing room, but there was another, far more important reason why we spent so much time in there. It was the only place in the whole school where you could listen to music . . . out loud.

And listen to music we did. Michael Jackson, Peter Gabriel, Joni Mitchell, Debbie Harry, Prince, Stevie Wonder, Pink Floyd. In the printing room we were free to dance around, to have fun. Free to enjoy ourselves. This was all so important, because listening to music was pretty much banned at Horris Hill. You were only allowed to listen to music for two hours on a Wednesday and Saturday and Sunday afternoon. All the other times your Walkman or stereo had to stay locked up in the stereo cupboard. I would get round this particular rule by hiding my Walkman in a plastic bag in the ceiling of one of the changing rooms. Then I would creep out into the woods and listen to the

Eurythmics, Lisa Stansfield, Joan Armatrading, The Beatles . . . Just like the printing room, this was my escape. A place where the teachers couldn't touch me. Hidden away in the woods, they couldn't control what I was hearing or understanding or thinking about. It was freedom.

The Gang

We were a funny group – me, Rupert, De Halpert (surnames only, remember), Castoro and Lewis . . .

Castoro was small and his dad was Italian; he was like the Danny DeVito of the playground. De Halpert was slightly taller, but he walked with a limp because one of his legs was shorter than the other. (He'd had an operation, which left him with an enormous scar running the length of one of his legs.) When he ran, the limp turned into more of a hop. He was quieter than the rest of us and a little bit more accident prone. Lewis was tall, and very gentle and shy. He was also very funny. None of them was remotely sporty and it was always fun to see the three of them move from their comfortable position of marauding the grounds as groundsmen or working in the swimming pool to attempting to kick a ball on a football pitch or trying to swing a cricket bat. Castoro, in particular, would defy anyone to laugh at him as he toe-punted another football onto the neighbouring pitch.

We were all great friends, especially in the summer term when we became the school's official groundsmen. The first job of the day was removing the swimming pool cover. The fun with this task was getting the chance to have a cheeky swim in the pool at the same time. This was a risky business because at any stage a passing teacher could simply pop his head over the fence and see any one of us paddling away, or hanging on to the end of the pool cover while we were dragged along in the water by the others. We also had to incorporate enough time to dry our hair, otherwise the game was up.

The other job that brought huge perks was delivering the 'cocoa'. This wasn't the drink, but the name for the food and drink handed out to the whole school on half-days, which were Wednesdays and Saturdays. It was normally iced buns or doughnuts along with two or three large urns of orange squash. The first bonus was that we could go and collect the food and drink from the kitchens, which often meant we had a chance to carry out a quick raid of the biscuit barrels. These were all unmarked containers, stashed high up on a top shelf. Due to our height, we could only just manage to flip up the lids and scoop our hands into the barrel, so it was pot luck what handful of biscuits we managed to grab. Our days were judged by our haul of biscuits. A good day – pink wafer or, my personal favourite, 'Nice' biscuits. A bad day – plain digestives or a chocolate Bourbon (I was never a fan, I'm afraid). Somewhere in the middle – fig rolls.

All this paled into insignificance, however, when we got our hands on the crates of iced buns or doughnuts that were entrusted to our charge. We would pile up the contents of our trolley and scoot off to the nearest corner, where we would sit for a while gorging ourselves on the cakes and guzzling strong orange squash (we would find the concentrate and double the ratio of squash to water). The problem was that each doughnut or bun was counted out so that every boy would get just one. No more, no less. We would end up eating about four each, which meant that by the time we got up to the cricket pavilion our stores were seriously depleted and so again the boys in the first year were forced to eat digestives and keep their mouths *shut*.

But then, one day, it all went horribly wrong. For some reason we decided to have a go at racing the trolley down the drive, which was very steep. It started off well but the trolley quickly careered out of control, De Halpert went flying, the urns jumped ship along with the iced buns, and Lewis rolled into a patch of brambles. Castoro – unusually nimble – performed a catlike leap and somersault and landed unscathed. I watched. The cocoa that afternoon was covered with grass and mud, and questions were asked. We were banned from using the trolley for quite a few weeks after that.

Smith

One event that took in the cricket pavilion, the swimming pool and most of the grounds and occurred every summer term was the Parents' Match. This was effectively our annual sports day. It was a tradition stretching back more than a century, with the main event being a match between the boys of the First Eleven cricket team and their fathers.

The day would start with athletics, then people would wander up to the main cricket ground, where the parents would park their cars around the pitch and get out their picnics. Like peacocks, they would arrive in their Bentleys or Range Rovers, Porsches or Ferraris, vintage cars or even the latest Rolls-Royce. Wicker hampers would be laid out, some parents creating quite a display for all to see with flower decorations and smoked salmon, while others hid meekly behind a sausage roll served out the back of a Morris Minor. De Halpert's parents would turn up in a modest estate car and park next to Mrs Castoro, who would always be in a fluster over where she could park, had she bought the right food, etc. . . . Lewis's parents would arrive, always very sweet and friendly. Finally, my own mum and dad would wander up with their picnic from my grandparents' house.

I certainly had a sense of not being among the glamorous, rich families. Our little group was on the edge really, operating in our own sphere – and that was okay by me. In fact, I wouldn't have had it any other way. With the family connection to the school, I guess I always felt pretty well protected in a way, and never really a part of the pomp and ceremony that can go on at these type of schools.

Whatever was going on around the cricket pitch, whoever had turned up with the latest Panama hat or priciest Barbour jacket, the newest Mercedes or the best Filipino maid, all and sundry came crashing down to ground level and presented a united front at the highlight of the day. The diving competition.

This was Mr Brown's chance to shine. He was the

ringmaster, the MC, the showman, the storyteller, the crusher of dreams and deliverer of life-long desires. For Mr Brown ran the swimming pool and, more importantly, he judged the diving competition. For the last twenty years at least Mr Brown had pulled on the same mustard-yellow swimming shorts (there is photographic evidence in the Horris Hill centenary book), stood opposite the springboard at the other end of the pool and set each contestant off on his planned dive. He would stand there in his shorts, hairy tummy hanging slightly over the waistband, soft, pudgy face pressed into a welcoming and encouraging smile. Mrs Brown would not be far away, adorned in a flowery-curtain number, watching her husband with fierce pride.

Mr Sudbury, Mr Brown's trusted sidekick, was deputy judge. He would not wear trunks, preferring a grey woollen suit. (God knows what he would have done if he'd had to jump in.) He was a small man – tiny, actually – with a little beard and he would always be holding a biro between his hands. He taught French and also ran the modelling room. (Rupert once came third in Mr Sudbury's modelling competition. He was making a model aeroplane when it collapsed, so he painted a piece of wood to look like a runway, placed the mangled plane on top and entitled it 'Crashed'. I thought it was one of the most genius things

I had ever seen.) Mr Sudbury was also in charge of the music for the school play and played the electric guitar. He was kind of cool, actually.

Slowly, as the time drew nearer to the diving competition, there would be a steady migration towards the pool. Some would walk and some would even drive, although the distance was only five hundred yards or so. Such was the desperation to get a prime place on one of the benches around the pool. Some parents, particularly the fathers, would stay outside the compound and peer in over the fence. Meanwhile I would put on my regulation swimming trunks along with the other boys and prepare myself – mentally and physically – for what lay ahead.

There were three stages to this yearly event. First, a standing dive from the springboard. Second, a little run and jump, also from the springboard. Third, a dive from the high board. This was the one that held the jeopardy. This was the one that the parents flocked to see.

The first two dives were expertly curated by Mr Brown from his position at the opposite end of the pool. He would stand there, clipboard in hand, as the diver waited for the signal. A little nod – and the dive would be performed. Then the second dive – wait, nod, dive. Then Mr Sudbury would take over for the third dive.

Although parents would give the pretence that they were rushing to get the best spot for their own darling child, all of them knew that really this was a smokescreen, a lie. There was really only one boy that everyone had come to see. The boy in question was known for being the worst diver in the school. Every year he would participate and every year his dives would be consistently awful. And when I say awful . . . this boy – let's call him Smith – never managed to get anywhere close to being vertical before entering the water. His body always remained crouched in a kind of arc and stayed like that as it smacked the water. He would fall like a stone every time. This is what the parents – especially the fathers – flocked to see really. Smith's spectacular belly flops. Every year Smith would stoically enter the diving competition and every year he held the entire school gripped.

Smith's First Dive

A silence descends on the compound as Smith prepares to take his first dive. And then the sound of a hundred cameras being unzipped from out of their bags. Some mothers are muttering between themselves and a father peering over the fence lights a cigar. Smith looks towards Mr Brown. Mr

Brown nods and smiles. Smith launches himself from the board. ('Launch' would be the wrong description actually. He essentially falls straight down from the end of the board.) A second later his body hits the water – face, arms and tummy all at the same time.

SMACK!

The soft but unmistakable sound bounces gently around the pool.

A little 'ooooh' comes out from the crowd.

Smith resurfaces, defiant. In his head, this dive has gone well. Could this be his year?

I don't think so, Smithy, I don't think so.

Smith's Second Dive

There have been some impressive dives. One boy manages a perfect swallow dive with the run and jump, another does a somersault. Bloody show-off. I scrape through, my legs coming slightly over the vertical as I enter the water. I don't care, high tea is awaiting and I have my eyes on the salami sandwiches.

A family is congratulating the smug parents of the somersault boy when Smith takes to the board. They stop mid-flow and turn back to the pool, eyes wide with anticipation. This time Smith is standing right at the beginning of the board to give himself as much room as possible to run and spring. I repeat, *to run* ... and then *spring*. Silence descends again. 'Every year,' one mother whispers to her neighbour. 'You'd think his parents would just take him home a day early.'

Smith looks for Brown, Brown finds Smith and gives him the nod and Smith is off. He runs along the board and springs elegantly into the air. Could this be the year? Has he been practising? Fathers are taking pictures frantically, mothers are looking hopeful. Even a baby stops crying.

Alas. Smith stops mid-air, mid-spring, and his body seems to shut down. Suddenly, it's like it's made of iron and there is just no way he can move it into a vertical position. He descends quickly, stomach parallel with the water, arms outstretched, face firmly planted between them.

SMAAAAAAAAAAACKKKKKKKK!

'Ooooohhhhhh.' A longer and deeper groan from the audience.

The baby starts to cry again, a few fathers are sniggering and slapping each other on the back. Even Mr Brown looks a bit perturbed.

Smith emerges, face still defiant. Proud. There is a small red mark on his tummy from the dive but he waves his mother away when she comes towards him with a towel. Smith is proud of his diving style.

Smith's Third Dive

And so the competition continues. The somersault boy manages a single pike from the high board. I fall from the board and manage some sort of entry into the water. Rupert's is pretty impressive. Another boy does a backwards dive. Wanker. His parents own a Bentley and – if the rumours are to be believed – half the school. If he isn't head boy next year, I'll do this competition naked. And then ... It's time.

Smith versus the high board.

Everything seems to go into slow motion. Smith walks towards the steps and ascends the ladder, rung by rung. With each step I can feel my heart pounding quicker and quicker. The fathers have now got their tripods out to give themselves the best chance of capturing the moment. More than one mother is crying, one has even run out of the swimming pool area sobbing, 'It's just so ... so *cruel*. He's not even aware he's shit.'

The air has become dense and Mr Sudbury, standing opposite the high board, is visibly shaking with the pressure. The fathers, on the other hand, are visibly shaking with silent laughter.

Up steps Smith. He's at the top. He looks around. From there he can see the tennis courts, the drive turning away lazily to the left down the hill, the cricket fields in the other direction and the common glimmering in the summer haze. A pair of swans fly overhead, looking for a place to settle. The last of the éclairs are being moved into the old gym for high tea while a lone rabbit lollops across the car park without a care in the world.

Smith hoists up his trunks, stretches his neck from one side to the other and assumes the position at the very edge of the high board.

I have actually stopped breathing, as has the entire crowd.

Mr Sudbury does his best to give Smith an encouraging smile as he lifts his head and gives him the all-important nod.

A whimper escapes a mother's mouth.

Smith falls. Like a stone. Like a pheasant that has been shot from the sky. Like a meteorite heading towards the earth. Smith falls towards the water. His face is meeting the water head-on, almost willing it to come towards him and then . . .

S M M M E E E E R R R R R A C C C C K-KKKKKKKKKKKKKKKKK!

'OOOOOOOOOOOOHHHHHHHHHHHHH-HHHHH.'

The sound of Smith's third dive and the subsequent cry of the audience carries all the way to the cricket pitch, where the groundsmen are setting up for the final twenty overs. A lady preparing high tea drops a plate of salami sandwiches (much to my dismay).

Smith emerges from the water. There is utter silence. No one speaks.

Then, suddenly, someone is clapping loudly and shouting, 'Bravo!'

It is Smith's father. Others begin to follow.

As Smith drags himself from the pool, more and more parents are applauding and shouting 'bravo' until the entire pool is on its feet and cheering. Smith looks around, smiling knowingly. To the dismay of the somersaulting and pike-diving boys' parents, there is only one true winner and everyone knows it. SMITH!

Miss Wakeley

'I've always regretted not playing an instrument,' my dad said to me when I was seven. 'Stick at it – you'll thank me one day. I promise.'

He was right. I can still play the piano a bit, and over the years it has helped me to find melodies and harmonies more quickly. Six years of lessons tuned my musical ear, I guess. More importantly, though, they allowed me to spend time with Miss Wakeley, my wonderful piano teacher.

Miss Wakeley was one of the few teachers at Horris Hill who I would say had a heart. A woman of generous build, she drove a lavender-coloured Ford Fiesta, had fine curly hair and wore a lot of floral. She walked with purpose, Miss

Wakeley: slowly and surely with a definite sit into both hips. Her left arm would come out to one side and swing across her body from front to back as if to balance her. She looked like a buoy bobbing along in the sea. You knew she would get there, but on occasion you worried for her safety.

Miss Wakeley played the clarinet and the organ as well as the piano. Famously, she almost came a cropper during a Sunday service one time. The school had just purchased a new organ with notes that could be played with the feet. So, in effect, there was a keyboard for the hands and another for the feet. To allow the player to swing up and down the foot keyboard, the stool would slide from left to right. There was also a button called 'tutti', which when pressed would crank the organ up to full blast. It was like the organ equivalent of a turbo charge. I resided on the back row of the choir (my voice was breaking) – nearest to the organ, along with my friends. This was the perfect place to get up to mischief without being spotted by the choir master. We would goad Miss Wakeley to hit that tutti button on every hymn.

'Go on, Miss Wakeley,' we would whisper during a service, 'hit the tutti. Tutti tutti tutti. Tutti frutti, Miss Wakeley!'

'Oh, now, boys – be *quiet!*' she would shush back. Eventually, though, she caved.

She was in the middle of Hymn 436, 'God Reside in Me', when after three verses of us urging her to hit the tutti button, she finally went for it. Unfortunately, she went for it while trying to play the keyboard in front of her and the one at her feet. As she hit tutti, she embarked on a slide from left to right. The organ jumped into turbo with such gusto that Miss Wakeley got a huge fright, and as a consequence pushed off far too hard into her slide. The stool propelled her towards the alto row – that was us – at one heck of a pace. She only just managed to grab on to the edge of the organ, which stopped her 1) from falling off the stool and 2) from squashing me and my alto colleagues to death.

Our shared near-death experience was eclipsed later that year by Mrs Stow, the old headmaster's wife, who occasionally filled in for Miss Wakeley. On one notorious Sunday she played the whole of Hymn 346 while the congregation sang what was actually the allotted hymn – Number 287.

Miss Wakeley had a novel way of entrapping a pupil while talking to him, particularly if he had missed his music lesson. On occasion, especially in the summer term, I would try to avoid my piano lesson. Now this was more complicated than it might seem. The big advantage of the summer term was that in break times you could play on the common, which was a maze of banks, bunkers, trees and hedges. We were extremely fortunate to have such a space. We would play games like British Bulldog and mass Kick the Can, and on occasions we would have a RIOT! This was an almost mythical institution at Horris Hill. Pupils remembered the riots of yesteryear. They were whispered about and expanded upon, the stories told and retold again until by the fifth time of telling, broken limbs, police and medics were involved.

A riot might happen once a summer term. A whisper would begin at tea time.

Castoro would turn to me over a particularly unpleasant cottage pie and say, 'Word is we are gonna have a riot.'

'No?' I say, while seeing if my food will actually stick to the underside of the table, thus defying gravity and allowing me not to eat it.

'That's the word. I'm gonna bring my hockey stick.' Castoro juts his chin in the manner of a Mafia hitman.

'But you don't own one.'

'Does this concern me, William?' And that would be that.

The younger boys would start to get nervous as soon as they heard the rumour. A riot meant them getting squashed, essentially. Smith the diver would try to secure his place in the sick bay, feigning a cough for Sister. His diving prowess wouldn't save him here. Any unpopular boy would try to avoid the common after tea, while others attempted a sort of camouflage with bits of bracken.

Grace would be said, the plates would be cleared, and then we would all head out onto the battlefield. There would be a minute's silence as we stood on the common awaiting our battle, with ourselves. You could feel the energy hanging in the air. We would eye each other up, friendships beginning to disappear, enemies coming to the foreground. We all became like lions, standing, watching for the weakest in the pack. Then someone, probably Castoro – with a tie around his head and wielding a hockey stick – would wail:

'RRRRIIIIOOOOOOTTTTTTT!'

And so it would begin.

Everything was a potential weapon. Frisbees, yo-yos, Rubik's cubes, rakes and dead branches. One hockey stick. Everyone would pile in. Friends would jump on each other and start pummelling. Groups of young boys would be rounded up and mown down. This all happened very, *very* quickly. There was a time limit, you see. It would take the teacher on duty about two minutes max to spot us, so we had to get in maximum pummelling time before the whole thing was called to a halt with the threat of extra prep.

As soon as the master on duty was alerted by the screams, thuds and the unmistakable sound of frisbees hitting shins, he would run to get reinforcements from the common room, where a few teachers might be contemplating the first whisky of the evening. Two or three disgruntled masters would emerge and that would be that. Just as quickly as the riot had started it would dissipate.

Some culprits would be named and shamed, and a universal fine might even be applied, like banning our ration of three boiled sweets on a Wednesday and Saturday or, even worse, banning our chocolate bar on a Sunday. Worst of all was the setting of lines. One hundred lines of 'I must not...' I was often tempted to insert 'I must not... have any fun at all at this school'. But the riot was worth all the ensuing punishments. It was worth the one or two minutes of release that it allowed us, the feeling of being free and letting out all of our pent-up aggression and frustration. Even if it did mean that sometimes Smith got his head kicked in.

Escaping injury in a common riot was hard, slipping past

Miss Wakeley to avoid a music lesson was nigh on impossible. To get to the common, you had to walk out of the boot room and sprint across the road. But the boot room was directly opposite the music room. Miss Wakeley would stand on the steps, eyes peeled in case any pupil attempted to escape a lesson or allotted music practice, which was assigned at the beginning of term, a minimum of two sessions a week. She would stand there with her coffee in one hand and the list for that day's roster in the other. Out the boys would spill and Miss Wakeley would pounce in a flash.

'De Halpert!' she would cry in her quivery voice. 'I believe you have a trumpet practice now. No, don't pretend you haven't heard me. De Halpert. DE HALPERT!'

She would catch them one by one as she sipped away on her coffee, her curly hair moving in the morning breeze as she barked out pupils' names. It was like a strange version of bingo. Truant bingo. Adventurous boys would try to sneak round the other way on to the common – out by the chapel and past the printing room. Miss Wakeley was wise to that, too.

'Saunders!' she would shout, seeing the boy to her left, even though her eyes were still scanning the boot-room exit. 'Yes, I see you Saunders. Piano practice *now*, if you please.' Saunders would mouth the question 'How?' as he slowly dragged his feet towards the music room. How indeed. She must have had the peripheral vision of an owl.

But if Miss Wakeley was impressive on the steps of the music room, she really came into her own in a one-on-one situation when you missed your music lesson.

I would be coming out of a Latin class and thinking of heading towards the dining room and lunch when she would appear from the other end of a long corridor.

'Young 1,' she would shout out in a determined way.

All would turn. Miss Wakeley would be standing there: flowery dress, tick; strong shoe with blocky heel, tick; right hand resting on hip and left hand wrapped across the body to rest lightly off her right hand, tick. Light coming from the window behind her so as to backlight her ample figure and gently stream through her soft hair, major tick. All the boys knew what would happen next. They'd seen the routine a hundred times before. The walk. Miss Wakeley would run her tongue over her teeth, purse her chapped lips, sigh out a breath of coffee and embark on THE WALK. Eyes fixed on her victim (me), her right hand would stay firmly planted on her hip while her left hand began to swing across her body, her top half swivelling clockwise and then back again with every couple of steps. The whole gait gave the impression of some sort of drunken yet purposeful sailor, doggedly determined to get to his target across the deck of a heavily pitching boat. Miss Wakeley was no sailor but she was most definitely heading for her target. Trembling slightly, I would watch, transfixed by this weaving, asp-like motion as she drew nearer and nearer.

Finally, she would arrive directly in front of me. This was when the circulating began. Hands on hips, she would deliberately plant her feet hip width apart. Then she would start to circulate her hips, slowly at first, as if doing the hula hoop. The circulating matched the words, which would always begin the same way.

'Young 1. Yoooooooooouuuuu (circulate, circulate) mis-ssssssed (circulate, circulate) yooooooouuuuuurrr (more circulating and getting faster) muuuuuusssssic lesssssssson' (finishing with quite vigorous circulating and a slight pant). While Miss Wakeley circulated she would also slowly shuffle nearer and nearer, so in the end you were literally backed into a corner. I was on the receiving end of this performance many times.

'But Miss Wakeley—'

'Ah, ah. No buts.' And the circulating would continue as she repeated, 'No buts, because yoooooooouuuuuuuuu missssssssed yoooooouuuuurrr muuussssssic lesssssson.'

This could go on for up to a minute – but it felt much

longer. And it always worked. After being entrapped by Miss Wakeley, I would not risk missing a music lesson again for at least half a term.

Miss Wakeley was, along with her oddities, one of 'the good ones'. She was kind. My parents always descended on her at Horris Hill teas because she was quite fun and we would play a game – who could give Miss Wakeley the last éclair. My other abiding memory of Miss Wakeley was her coming out of the teachers' loo having tucked her dress into her rather large bloomers. A teacher called Mr Goldsworthy, seeing her predicament, stalked her down the corridor and snapped the dress out of her knickers outside the senior French class in C1.

Miss Wakeley turned round to confront her assailant and screamed, 'Michael! What are you doing?'

To this day, I cannot forget the look of shock and horror on both of their faces.

Sweet Rations

Another reason why I loved Miss Wakeley was because she would let me eat sweets that I had smuggled into the school during her lesson. As I mentioned, we weren't allowed sweets at Horris Hill except for Wednesdays, Saturdays and Sundays. On Wednesdays we were handed three boiled sweets, fruit salads or black jacks. I can still remember the disappointment as the three black jacks were slammed down on the table in front of me. Saturdays were the same but on Sundays we were allowed a full chocolate bar! (I should say at this point that after the initial two years of being a day boy, I then became a fully fledged boarder. This meant we only saw our parents four days a term. Everyone else was doing it, so I think that is why Rupert and I also did it. It was kind of simple as that.) On Saturdays and Sundays we were also played classical pop in the dormitories, so weekends really were a riot!

The lack of sweets gave a whole new significance to meetings with our parents. These meetings were important because they gave us a chance to get some much-needed love and affection. They also provided an opportunity to replenish our supplies of sweets. This was strictly illegal, of course, so all these banned gifts would have to be hidden as soon as we returned to the dorms. I would take the batteries out of my torch and cram gummy bears or jelly babies into the empty space. I would hollow out large dictionaries and keep my Twixes and Marathon bars in them.

I would stuff my crisps into a tennis ball can, leaving just one ball at the top so if a master looked in he would never suspect. I even once made a map of where I'd hidden my Lion bar in the woods.

My favourite hiding-place was under a loose floorboard in Dormitory 11 in the main school. This was a tricky one because Dorm 11 was right above the common room, so you ran the risk of being heard by the teachers. The risk was worth it, though, because under the floorboards lay a Tupperware box overflowing with pink prawns, banana sweets, strawberry lips, cola worms, fizzy cola bottles, love hearts, flying saucers and chocolate peanuts. But then, one day – tragedy. Without warning, the old floorboards were covered with new carpets. I sometimes wonder if my Tupperware box of sweets still resides under the carpet that was laid in Dorm 11 back in 1992.

Of course, the school was well aware of the secret transactions that occurred between parent and child on the limited occasions when they were allowed to interact on school property. So tuck-box raids or desk searches would often be carried out after the weekend of the school concert or the school play, when parents would come and watch the show and you got to hang out with them for at least three hours.

The concert itself was terribly boring and the highlight for most people was the school tea afterwards. My highlight, however, was watching Miss Wakeley tackling the clarinet in the school orchestra. Other teachers cropped up there, too: Mr Brown lounged in the back row with his violin; Mrs Wainwright-Maxwell was in the front, which gave the dads something to look at; and Mr Sudbury, who as mentioned played the electric guitar, also played the bassoon. (I mean . . . *what?*) Actually this man was a genius for he also played an array of recorders and the piccolo, which was so *tiny*. Like him! I loved it when he would ever so calmly swap between each instrument. He would lay down his bassoon – with Mr Brown playing the same two notes that he had been playing for the last thirty years – pick up his recorder and then deftly place that down on his music stand and, quick as a flash, reach inside his jacket pocket and take hold of his piccolo. It was extremely impressive.

As I said, though, my favourite part of the concert was watching Miss Wakeley on the clarinet. As you might expect from the school's music teacher, she always featured prominently throughout the concert. She ran the junior choir. She played in the orchestra. And often she would accompany a soloist, if a little clumsily. God, I loved that woman.

Afterwards, there would be a chance to wander around the various activities the school offered, so you were encouraged to show your parents the new squash courts or the new art room, along with the more staple activities such as Mr Brown (violin still in hand) at the train room and Mr Sudbury (what does this man not do?) at the modelling room *and* the new photography lab!

There were many bad points about the school, and you may wonder why my parents sent me there. From their point of view, though, they sent me to a place that had the best facilities out of almost any of the prep schools in the UK. It really was incredibly impressive. To know how to develop our own photographs before the age of thirteen; to be coached in squash and tennis; to have such wonderful grounds to play (and riot) in. To have a swimming pool and print room, state-of-the-art science and arts rooms, a sports hall with an enormous stage for school plays (which were always fantastic and started my love of acting and singing). To have an athletics track and beautiful cricket, football and rugby pitches.

All of this was a dream for a little boy's education, and my parents gave up a lot to send me there. They did what they thought was right and the gaps and eccentricities gave me some experiences that were fun to rally against.

It was fun to hide sweets. It was fun to try to sneak in a swim before charging around on the cocoa trolley. It was fun playing the mad games that were invented by the school. It was fun bonding with my friends in the printing room, listening to Pink Floyd. A lot of these things provided me with happy memories. But a lot of other things did not.

For instance, because of the illicit sweet-smuggling trade, when you had a birthday you would have to be watched over by someone when your parents visited. A birthday was managed by the school like a well-rehearsed military operation. Your parents would arrive after lunch and would be let into the headmaster's house, on the 'private side'. Meanwhile, you were told to sit outside the headmaster's office, on the 'school side', and wait for the red light to turn to green. Once the light changed you were allowed to go through to the dining room, where your parents would be waiting. With the head matron. This was to check that nothing 'illegal' changed hands – sweets or inappropriate presents, such as banned toys, or maybe a sub-machine gun, hardcore porn or perhaps some acid tabs that you had prearranged a killer price for from the ten-year-olds.

It was awful and sad and awkward to be in a room and feel guilty to receive a hug from your mum or a kiss from your dad. To open a present and then immediately be told you couldn't have it and it would have to be taken home. I even felt aware of what I was saying and unfortunately I wasn't yet proficient in Morse code (although I bet the matron was) and my parents couldn't lip read to the point that they could understand the sentence: 'They are all FREAKS in here, get me out and let's do home education.'

I always wanted my parents to arrive with the most inappropriate presents. Like a baby crocodile or a stripper. They could then have turned to the matron and said: 'Sorry? What do you mean we can't give William a rent boy for his thirteenth birthday? What if we remove his three-piece suit made of cocaine? I suppose these new nunchucks are out of the question, then?' Examples of banned presents included remote-controlled cars, clothes and roller-skates. Certain board games were considered dangerous enough to incite anarchy. A new bike – even a new football – was completely out of the question, too.

It was ridiculous. Over time, because of our family 'links' to the school, Rupert and I managed to get our present openings moved to my parents' car in the car park. At least we could hug there without feeling judged.

Another sticky area was the birthday cake. Now mine and Rupert's cakes were always very special. They were made by the Polly Tea Rooms in Marlborough and they would always represent something we had all experienced as a family. One year a teacher called our cakes 'ostentatious' because they were made to look like cheeseburgers from a burger joint we visited on days out with our parents. Another boy's cake was banned because it had 'too many sweets on it', and was replaced with one of the plain school cakes you got if your parents didn't come to visit on your birthday. Can you believe that some kids didn't even get to see their parents on their birthday?

Cecil Star

Horris Hill was famous for its great theatre productions. Of course, as it was an all-boys school, cross-dressing was involved. In my first role I played one of Cleopatra's fair maidens. (I remember sitting at the side of her throne thinking to myself, *It should have been me. I should be Cleopatra.*) The following year I played the show-stealing role of Cecil Star, the camp director. For my opening entrance I had to burst in, run over to Mr Inus the headmaster, and sit on his knee. A daring feat in itself to sit on Skinny Inny.

It was at this stage that I really started to dream of becoming a singer and performer. The plays gave me validation for the very first time. I remember my godmother's daughter Annabel, who was so glamorous and wonderful, telling me, 'You know, that really was *very* good! You do know that, don't you? Because you should.' I hadn't known until then – but now I did begin to get an inkling . . . and that gave me the confidence to dream.

There are so many more stories I could tell of Horris Hill. Its oddities, the strange teachers and their even stranger ways. The wonderful moments that could only have occurred within such an archaic institution, along with the not-so-great times that I have been fortunate to survive and, over time, find peace with.

Horris Hill was an extremely odd school but it was there, in the sports hall, running around as a camp director, that I started to formulate a sense of where I wanted to go in life, and who I wanted to be. It began as the kernel of an idea, a seed of belief that gestated in the back of my mind and in my heart over the next six years. It was always there in my hopes and my imagination as the 'thing that needs to happen'. It was the dream that needed to be fulfilled. Who knew that it would take a new talent show that broke the mould in so many ways to make that thing happen?

Second row at Burberry

'Should you even be going?' Michael asks me.

We are sitting in a café in London Fields. I have ordered three coffees in a row because Michael fancies the waiter but doesn't want to drink or eat anything. It is London Fashion Week. I am pumped so full of caffeine my head is shaking.

'Well,' I say. 'It *is* Burberry. I mean, they are the best sort of show at London Fashion Week, no? I think it could be quite exciting. *No?*'

'Well, yeah,' he concedes, 'it will be exciting. But...' He adopts the position of a young primary-school teacher who has just found a five-year-old with a cut knee. 'You are *second row.*'

'Second row,' I whisper, acknowledging the crime.

'Second row.'

'Second row,' I repeat.

Michael leans forward. 'Second—'

'All *right*, I get it! Second row! I get it! It's not bad, is it? I mean – it's only one back from first row.'

Michael breathes in . . .

'*Don't* say the word again. Please.'

He shrugs and cranes his neck to look for the handsome waiter. 'It could give off the wrong message, that's all I'm saying. You turn up, and there you are, seated behind a younger, prettier, less puffy version of yourself.'

'Thanks.'

'My pleasure. People see you, they see old, they see has-been, they see washed up. Words like "veteran" pop into their heads. And suddenly, before you know it, there you are sashaying across the ice in a spangly one-piece, skating for your life in the *Dancing on Ice* skate-off.' Michael sighs and shakes his head. 'It's just something to think about. Now go and order another coffee from our handsome friend.'

'Michael, if I order another coffee I am actually going to start convulsing.'

'Do it anyway. It'll make me look more attractive.'

I order another coffee.

Now what Michael is airing is something I was worrying about myself. In the last ten years I have been to just two fashion shows. The first was for Matthew Williamson in New York. I was running from a broken heart and potential breakdown that took me to Los Angeles, Thailand, back to Los Angeles, on to New York for the show, and then back home to the UK for the breakdown.

I sat opposite Anna Wintour, who was drinking a Starbucks. I asked the chic lady who showed me to my seat if I could get what Ms Wintour was having. I said it as a joke. The chic lady didn't laugh. (It wasn't very funny.) The girls were very skinny and the clothes were amazing and at the time I didn't realise what a thing it was to sit in the front row. It was fun and I ended the day dancing with a dwarf.

For my second fashion show experience I went to see an

Issa show with four of my friends. I was asked to sit in the front row next to Daisy Lowe and a model I hadn't heard of. I didn't understand as I wanted to sit with my friends, so I asked if one of them could come up to join me. This was met with a negative (understandably), so I stayed in the fifth row and watched the show from there. At the time I thought it was a bizarre concept to sit away from your friends just to be 'seen' in the front row, squashed between two people you didn't know. Now I realise it's quite a privilege, even if you do get squashed.

And so now we arrive at Burberry – my third show and the biggest. The daddy of British fashion shows, in fact. This has not happened by chance. My publicist has arranged for me to be invited to the shows this year and the corresponding parties. And here I have it – a ticket! A golden ticket to the big one: BURBERRY! I am genuinely excited. Christopher Bailey is not only one of the best designers but also one of the most eligible gay men in the world. He's been chief creative officer at Burberry for over ten years, transforming it from a rather stuffy label that people looked down on to the crème de la crème of high fashion. He mixes creativity with consumerism to perfection and the shows are exciting.

I am fresh from a yoga weekend and so zenned up to the

eyeballs I'm actually floating towards the show in a Margiela jumper, jodhpur-like trousers and shiny black shoes. I have gone 'low-key' fashion. I've gone, 'Oh *this* old outfit? I just threw it on in two minutes,' when in truth my bed back home is covered with a mountain of clothes ranging from old capes to an all-in-one romper suit. (I thought it could have grabbed headlines.)

I arrive at the event and it is thrilling. My nerves are outweighed by the scale of the show, which is being put on in a transparent marquee next to the Prince Albert statue in Hyde Park, opposite the Royal Albert Hall. Everything has been organised and created with exquisite attention to detail. The floor surrounding the marquee is brilliant white and radiates a pleasant and forgiving light when the stars arrive to be photographed. The front end of the marquee is layered in a deep grey textured wall made up of overlapping rectangles. It is stunning.

I walk up the line of press.

'Why are you here, Will?' asks a guy from morning television.

'I am modelling the clothes,' I reply.

The guy laughs.

I look at him with a deadpan gaze. 'Why are you laughing?'

He stops mid-laugh. 'Serious?'

I approach the camera in a clandestine fashion and whisper, barely audible, '*Deadly*,' then turn on my heel headlong into a teenage fashion blogger from Japan, who asks me who I am. I tell her I am Jesus. She asks me what Jesus is wearing. I say usually a minimal Comme des Garçons cloak, but today I've injected some colour and lost the sandals. I could have gone on for some time and am about to explain what the disciples would be wearing (if they were here), but a Japanese girl band has arrived and I am literally elbowed aside by my interviewer, who brushes me away with her microphone, which has a bright yellow foamy head. She is, in fact, striking me repeatedly with the microphone to get me to move, like a farmer attempting to move a cow. It is very funny. I move on before she kills me, and head into the marquee.

There is a sea of canvas stools either side of a gleaming white runway that stretches seamlessly to a textured geometric wall at the back, echoing the pattern at the front. It's all rather beautiful, and it doesn't stop at the furniture. People. Fashionable people of all shapes and sizes litter the marquee. Fantastic outfits, stunningly gorgeous men and women and some not so gorgeous but still with a flair and a desire to express themselves however they choose. People are air kissing and glancing over each other's shoulders. Star spotting is the primary pastime. I see a blonde, skinny, pretty Hollywood actress. I am not sure who she is, but I remember seeing her at the theatre once. There is the actor Eddie Redmayne, the incredible-looking model Rosie Huntington-Whiteley . . . the list continues. But the biggest celeb is yet to come and if I knew what I was about to do next I think I might have sprinted out of the show there and then.

As I move slowly towards my *second row* seat my phone vibrates.

It's Michael. 'Are you in?'

'Hello to you, too. And yes, I'm in. I'm not a spy, you know.'

'Okay . . . well. Well done. Who's there? What are you wearing? Are you wearing white? You always wear white. I bet you're wearing white.'

'I'm not wearing white.'

'I knew you wouldn't wear white. Grey? Surely not green?'

'Shall we go through every colour of the spectrum, Michael?'

'It's okay, I've found you on the webcam. Margiela. Nice. Possibly a bit dress down. Anyway – have you seen her?'

'Webcam? What are you, fashion's Big Brother? And I'll need a little bit more to go on than "her".'

'*Her.* Have you seen . . . *her?*'

'Oh, *her.* Oh well, yes of course I've seen *her.* No, I have not seen *her*, Michael, I have no idea who you are talking about and I am kind of busy trying to . . . look busy,' I hiss out in a projected whisper.

'Oh, God, do I have to spell *everything* out to you? Anna Wintour. I mean, you do know who she is, no?'

'Yes, thank you, I do know who Anna Wintour – The Most Famous Magazine Editor in the World – is. And no, I haven't seen *her.*' I pause. 'Actually, do you think she'll be here? Ooh, that's exciting! I'm gonna look for her.'

'Wait, *wait.* William? Are you definitely second row?'

'Yes, Michael. I am second row. I'm heading there now.'

He sighs with resignation. 'You poor thing. God speed, my friend. God speed.'

I put the phone back in my pocket and look for my seat with renewed vigour, keeping a close eye out for the icon that is Anna Wintour. When I reach my seat I discover that I'm sitting next to Dan Gillespie Sells from The Feeling. He's a friend, so this is good. More and more people are coming in now – all the fashion students are crammed into the back row on either side of the catwalk. It makes me realise how much they would kill to be in the second row. I'm lucky. I'm not front row, but I'm still lucky.

The show is about to start ... and then I see her. The crowds have parted and I see the full glory that is The Wintour almost opposite me – front row and centre, of course. She is in delicate colours; loose light cotton trousers and a long flowery shirt. Do not be deceived, though. This is no Laura Ashley look. It's directional yet comforting, thought-out yet effortless. It's Anna Wintour and she looks fucking fabulous. With massive sunglasses on.

I am beginning to experience an out-of-body sensation. Suddenly my right arm is twitching and lifting up of its own accord. She is looking over my way. Consciously, I am trying to stop my arm from rising. Subconsciously, my mind and body are saying, 'I know her, we are friends, I *need* to let her know I'm here.' My arm continues to rise slowly and I whisper to Dan, 'Anna Wintour is looking our way. You know what she's thinking, don't you?'

'Who is that gay boy in pastel Margiela?'

'No, Dan. She is thinking ... cover star.'

At this point my arm reaches its full height and I begin a slow, determined wave in Anna Wintour's direction. I couple this with a sort of meek tight-lipped smile, where just the corners of my mouth turn up, which makes me look like a slightly deranged zombie. The first lady of fashion's gaze does not linger on me, so my wave becomes more frantic.

'Will! What are you doing?' Dan mutters in my ear.

'Waving at Anna Wintour,' I reply, dreamily.

'Why?'

'Er . . . I don't actually know,' I say, in my dreamy tone. 'I am going to stop now.' I put my arm down. Suddenly I awake from my zombie-like state and realise what I have done.

WHAT HAVE I DONE?

I have just waved, in a hugely pervy, odd manner. At Anna Wintour. Oh, God.

I really don't think she noticed. She didn't notice. And no one else would really notice, they would just think I was waving at a fashionista friend across the way. I begin to calm. This is okay. A moment of madness that has passed and now I can enjoy the show.

My phone vibrates. It's a text from Michael.

'Why the FUCK are you waving in that weird way? And WHO are you waving at? STOP IT. NOW. IT'S WEIRD. PS: have you seen her????'

I text back. 'I have just waved at Anna Wintour. As if I knew her. I want to cry. Or be sick. Or both.'

A ten-second pause. Then:

'WHAAAAAAAAATTTTTTTT?'

Then another text:

'I mean WHAAAAAAAATTTTTTTTT??? YOU DID WHAAAAAAAAATTTTTTTTTTTTTTT?????????'

I turn my phone off and put it in my pocket. I shall not reply. I shall also, possibly, after the show, bury myself in Hyde Park and lie there for the rest of eternity.

The music starts and the first model steps onto the cat-walk to gasps of delight and a look of satisfaction on the face of the editor of American *Vogue*.

My new friend.

'I would like a cell with a view, please'

I was retaking my A levels in Oxford. Another statistic: public schoolboy flunked his exams at £10,000 a year private school; went on a mini-gap year (pronounced 'gaaaap yeeaaar', if you're posh); and then got Daddy to pay for private sixth-form college and rent him a flat so he could pass his exams and go to university.

The frustrating thing is, I worked really hard for my A levels. Too hard. I flunked them because I overworked and no one really taught me how to take an exam. It sounds as if I still have sour grapes. (Perhaps I do!) Either way, I spent six months living in Oxford, relearned the syllabus and ended up with an A in Ancient History and another in Politics to add to the B grade I already had in English.

While studying in Oxford, I lived in a flat in Summertown, an area largely populated by people in their eighties. Sometimes between seminars I would nip home in my Mini, which I loved and cherished, to grab some more books. As I knew I would only be a few minutes max, I didn't always park in my allotted parking space. However, some of the residents of Roger Street Apartments were *extremely* vigilant about who parked where, as I soon learned. For even in this brief space of time, the old lady who lived above me would spot that I had parked in the wrong space. She would then somehow manage to get down a flight of stairs, place a passive-aggressive note on my windscreen, and still get back up to her flat in time to watch me dash out to my car, over-laden with files and books, and find the said note. The most incredible thing about this whole manoeuvre was that she walked with a Zimmer frame. After reading the note, I would turn in disbelief towards the flats and see her standing at her window, leaning on her Zimmer, gazing down at me in silent triumph.

One morning, when she had been especially quick in her note-placing mission, I looked up at her in amazement, then bowed in respect. She watched me with a deadpan expression, although I could have sworn I saw a tiny smirk creep across her lips. I honestly think I must have been living underneath Supergran.

I could have done with Supergran one early summer night, when I engaged in a disastrous event that left me banned from driving for eighteen months. The weekend before, I had gone up to London for a night out. I would often drive up and back the same night from Oxford. Many of my friends were indeed on their 'gaaaap yeeaaarrs' but some were still knocking around and on this particular Friday night I ran into my ex-girlfriend, Amy.

It was around this time that I was beginning to confront the fact that I was definitely gay. I would sit in my flat and think, How the fuck am I going to deal with this? It seemed such an insurmountable obstacle. I was so terrified

of going to a gay club, being seen near a gay club or even thinking about it.

I had heard of a gay night at the Fridge in Brixton, one of those passing comments that would go something like: 'Oh, yeah, the Fridge has a good night on a Sunday. It's full of poofters, though, so keep your backs to the wall.' My ears would prick up. A gay night? There is actually a gay night somewhere that I now know about? It just seemed so exotic and surreal – an exciting yet terrifying land that I could never, *ever* really go near. I remember this one time leaving a club in Chelsea where I used to hang out. It was about one o'clock in the morning. I wasn't drinking at that time, so I would drive back to Oxford or my parents' house the same night. I remember sitting in my car, thinking, Go on . . . drive to Brixton. Do it now. You can do it. Just turn the car round, head to Brixton, find the Fridge, and go in.

I was actually talking out loud to myself when a friend from school drove past and stopped to ask if I was all right. Even then I was terrified that he might have an inkling of what I was thinking. I said I was fine and off I drove.

For years, I had been trained, conditioned, to hide any notion that I might be gay. I am aware that this sounds ridiculous, having written about prancing around playing a camp director, but I went into survival mode when I entered the sixth form. I became hyper-aware of never seeming like I might be gay. This is why I dated a girl in my last year. To call someone gay was one of the biggest insults you could say to another boy. It was a framework of utter shame that unfortunately still operates in schools today, and it saddens and maddens me greatly that both schools and the government continue to gloss over the use of 'gay' as a derogatory term.

So much has changed in terms of racial equality and awareness of different religions, but to be a gay boy or girl is still seen as open ground for young people to ridicule.

This was the climate I lived in as a young gay boy. Within school and wider society, gay was wrong. Simple. There were very few gay pop stars really (not out, anyway), and those who were out were considered wrong and disgusting. I grew up in the era of the Aids epidemic and how was this disease portrayed in the media? The evil GAY DISEASE. Gays caused it. Gays go on marches and gays get beaten up. Gays are bad and wrong – that was the message I heard as a teenager – loud and clear.

I knew deep down from a very young age that I was gay and there was no suitable role model to follow. In many ways I think my generation were the last who really were punching in the dark in terms of gay identity.

Because of all this, I learned to completely cover up any notion of being gay. I remember staying at a friend's house in Cornwall after A levels when a really cute boy turned up to visit. He wore a suede coat and flares. I owned some suede flares. It should have been a match made in heaven. He stayed the night and some of my friends made fun of him behind his back, saying he was gay. I remember one friend saying, 'I mean, did you see how he crossed his legs? Like a woman! Like a gay!'

I *did* notice that and there is one thing about being gay – you know the signs of another gay man from ten paces. Of course you do – you walk in your own shoes, so you are going to spot the gay tread of someone else. This boy was really sweet and took a shine to me while I was listening to music in my Mini with some friends. I ridiculed him in front of my mates. I didn't want anyone even remotely connecting me to him. The sad, deeper truth was I actually really wanted the opposite. I wanted to cop off with this kindred spirit, but I was too scared and terrified of how people would react. Afterwards, I was so ashamed of the way I had treated him.

Girls were as bad as boys, by the way. I remember a girl once calling me gay because I was wearing a flowery shirt. (She was on the money.) My friends went ballistic. I can't tell you how awful it felt when she shouted those words. It was as if she had caught me out. That's still how it's often portrayed in the media, in fact. You read it in the papers – 'So and so "admits" to being gay'. *Admits?* Why admits? As if they are guilty of wrongdoing – even today.

We have, however, come a long way. Back in my teens I was not able to confront my huge fear and shame of being gay, so I would still go out in London pretending to eye up girls. And when I ran into my ex-girlfriend Amy, I thought, This could be an opportunity to have another go at straightening myself out! I asked her down to Oxford.

The next week Amy arrived and we went out to the pub and then on to a club. As we left the club to go home, I decided to drive the short distance from Cowley Road to Summertown. That was not a good idea because I was considerably over the limit. Somehow I managed to get us back to the flat and drop Amy off. It was then that I decided to go out again for a final drive to get a doner kebab. I could have walked to the kebab van – in fact it would have been quicker that way. This didn't stop me. I turned left into the street and headed up towards the doner van, driving the wrong way up a one-way street. It was okay . . . there were no cars . . . until a police car turned in at the top. Oh, crap. In my confused state I thought I could just creep past them and quickly turn back down my street, park up, and all would be fine. Such was my drunken delusion. I whizzed into the car park and still took the time to parallel park and in my allotted space, in case Supergran was lingering upstairs. The police, of course, followed and the blue lights arrived flashing as they pulled up next to me.

One of the policemen came round. I wound down my window.

'Would you get out of the car please, sir?'

'Of course, Officer.' Act sober, act sober. You can do this. I opened the door and it seemed to stop. It was stuck.

I opened it a few more times, panic rising. Something was in the way.

'Ha ... I'm *awfully* sorry, Officer,' I drolled in my most nonchalant, sober voice. 'The door seems to be stuck.' I continued to slam it out as hard as possible.

The officer's hand rested on the door. 'That's because you're slamming it against the car next to you, sonny,' he said.

In my haste I had parked so closely to the MG sports car next to me that I was actually wedged in against it. I had been slamming continuously against its front passenger door.

'I'll repark!' I announced, still believing I could win this one.

I reparked and opened the door.

As I began to get out, the officer asked, 'Have you been drinking, sir?'

'No ... oooooooo,' I protested, my reply becoming more of a shriek as my foot caught on the seat-adjustment lever for my racing bucket seat I was so proud of. I crashed to the ground.

'Give it up, son, give it up.'

My face was resting against the cold wet tarmac. It was nice and so I decided to shut my eyes and maybe have a little nap. 'Night, night, Officer ...'

The next thing I knew, I was lying in a police cell on the other side of town. The two policemen were actually hysterical. I had done some serious modelling poses for my official criminal record photos. (Actually I would pay good money to see them.) I was wearing my second-hand suede jacket, so the guys kept calling me Jarvis.

'Is our daddy rich, Jarvis?'

'I like your Mini, Jarvis. You won't be needing that any more!'

It was all tongue in cheek.

I told them my papa was a multi-millionaire (not true, of course) and demanded a cell with a view. I was four times over the limit and so far gone that I think they found me amusing. I also heard myself saying that I would be famous one day. I would be a famous singer and they should all remember me! I wonder if they did.

They were so decent they actually dropped me back home later that night, even though they should have kept me in. My favourite moment was the next day when the officers turned up in the evening and one of them offered to buy my Mini. He said his wife was looking for a little runaround!

The episode continued. I ended up missing my court date, so a warrant was issued for my arrest. I came back to

Oxford and walked into a police station to be arrested. They handcuffed me and drove me across the street to court in an armoured police van, with my feet shackled to the floor. Then they held me in a cell after removing my tie and shoelaces.

While I was waiting for sentencing they brought in another prisoner, who was being tried for stealing a car and driving without a licence as well as being over the limit. He mentioned his girlfriend was coming in too. I said that was nice, and he said, yeah, it was her day to be tried too – she was coming in from Reading prison. I suggested he did a secretarial course in Gloucester Road in Kensington because that was what a lot of my friends did and they found it very useful. Either that or the three-month introductory course at Prue Leith's cookery school. Our communication broke down after that.

After all this I was quite rightly banned from driving for eighteen months and given a hefty fine.

I learned a lot of lessons from this experience. 1) Don't drink and drive, obviously – it's stupid and reckless. 2) Secretarial lessons aren't for everyone. 3) Watch out for the bucket seat-adjustment lever on old Minis. But the thing that really stuck with me was this. All that time during the night of my arrest, my ex-girlfriend Amy was back at my flat, waiting for a night of action. And I had chosen to abandon her, get into a car and drive – dead drunk – the wrong way down a one-way street in search of a kebab.

If there was ever a sign that I was definitely on the gay side of the tracks, surely this was it. So I vowed to myself that whatever happened, with licence or without, drunk or sober, university was going to be the place where I bit the bullet and would finally come out.

It makes me think of the old proverb: 'A gay man on foot is worth two straight men in a Mini.'

I live with this as a mantra.

Down and out?

This week has not been a good week. In fact, it has taken a lot to get myself to write at all.

I suppose this is as good a time as any to talk of my depression. At present I feel lost. Energy is low. The future seems blank to me (a bit like this page). I am not excited, I am not hopeful, I am not content with myself. I experience sudden, huge waves of emotion, of feeling entirely desolate, panicky and trapped, as if there is no way out. It takes all my strength to remain calm and focused. I feel anaesthetised, numb and cold.

I know these feelings. When I wake up I just want to stay in bed. It takes a monumental effort to heave myself out and start the day. I would rather lie in bed and allow my mind to wander until it has found a kernel of self-doubt, something to grab on to and nurture, which within barely a minute has become a full-blown menace. Reminding me why there is no point and why I really am a severely shit person.

I have to do things to remind myself I am alive. Running is proving helpful at the moment. I am training to do a marathon and it is good to get out in the Welsh countryside and feel the cold air, feel the energy returning to my body.

It's now thirteen years since I first became truly aware that I suffer from depression. The weird thing is that it's partly thanks to my depression that I have managed to stay so sane. These inner feelings of worthlessness mean that I have never been swept away into that crazy place of worrying constantly about what the papers or people say, because I have either concurred or thought, Is that all you've got? I could do better – *much* better – myself! When I first started, my opinion of my work and my singing was often so low that it really didn't matter what critics said about the show or my songs or me as a person . . . because I had already thought all of it myself.

The one thing that has got me through, though, the one thing that has remained sacred, is my love of singing. I was damned if I would ever get to a point where I would screw up my chances of having a pop career. Because singing is my way of reconnecting with the true me, the powerful me, the me that has a core belief of being good. It teaches me to trust my instincts, be in the moment and allow myself to make decisions naturally. It's like a safety valve that stops my depression from ever sabotaging my work.

This bad patch has been triggered by a run-in with my ex-boyfriend. I was feeling rather barren anyway and decided to hit the ground running by starting to smoke again after six weeks of not. Good for the self-esteem. I then proceeded to drink too much. It was sad because I had just exchanged on my house and yet I was feeling nothing. No happiness. No elation. The day before I had been so excited but suddenly all that positivity vanished. So I went to a well-known gay pub in the East End and managed to improve my mood with a couple of friends. Things were on the up.

Next I met an old beau who was still looking great and that perked me up some more. But then the ex appeared. Within five minutes I was a tequila shot down and asking him to go out with me again... after a three-year gap. All of my pride had evaporated.

The long and the short of it was that this was a trigger. On the drive down to Wales, I wanted to turn back to London at least ten times. The idea of being with other people was terrifying but I also knew it was the best thing to do. There is a desire to isolate yourself when you are depressed and it is the worst thing you can do. It has taken me years of therapy to learn to fight this urge and plough on. And ploughing on is what I have done this week. It is a fight, minute by minute. Even in my current state I feel proud of this achievement. I see progress. My self-esteem has not dipped too low. I still feel okay about myself – but there is just a general feeling of malaise.

There is some thinking that needs to be done: about the ex, about my inability to move on, and about my overall uncertainty in matters of the heart. There is always something to learn, but this week I have had to put battle armour on just to exist. Get up, eat, run, socialise, keep busy, maintain a routine and 'get on with it'. I go to bed at 10 p.m. at the latest, and I am knackered.

But it's getting better now. My head is lifting from the fog a little. I think of next week and I can smell some lightness, feel a sense of excitement about the projects coming up – of which there are many – and I think: Perhaps I have managed this turn rather well. Whereas before it would be months of up and down, this has been six days. I noticed the trigger, I saw the signs, and I fought back. Come tomorrow I will be more on the up and come next week I will look back and see that I have managed to survive and work at the same time.

This is the goal – not to let this disease get on top of me. Hang on to the knowledge that I can get through it. I have been down this week but not out. Oh no. And, to be honest, the idea of that is too awful to bear. It conjures up images of months in bed; utter hopelessness. It strips so much pleasure away from things – even those little everyday things, because every day can be an utter pleasure. The trick is to force your brain into remembering this. That life can be fun and a pleasure – and slowly, this knowledge drips down into you and calms you down again.

The way I see it is, I have this thing that takes hold of me. I can often see and understand the reasons but my response is an overreaction. This can be a positive trait – it makes me sensitive to things, it probably allows me to sing and perform the way I do. So I have to learn to live with it and I am lucky because I can get the best help.

Not everything can be perfect in life. I have things that I still can't get right. Love and relationships terrify me; I remain heartbroken for years – but in a way this gives me the creative drive for what I do.

Depression tries to steal your happiness. If you take away happiness you have nothing. So I am determined to fight on – because you only live once and I intend to spend as little time as is humanly within my reach feeling like that.

Boy band auditions this way

It's September 2001. I am down to the last fifty on *Pop Idol*.

There had never been a show like it before. A competition to find a singer. One solo act. It had been preceded by a show called *Popstars*, which was a search to put together a group. That had been a huge success, but the genius of *Pop Idol* was to put the responsibility of choosing

the winner in the public's hands. That was the big twist –
the public would vote for the person they thought should
win, not the judges.

Pop Idol appeared at a time when manufactured pop was
rife. From Britney Spears to S Club Seven, Westlife to
B★Witched, the TV was chock-full with pop acts who
didn't write their own songs, said what they were told to
say and often didn't even sing live. The sight of a pop star
or group miming badly on music shows such as *CD:UK*
and *Top of the Pops* was commonplace. *Pop Idol* was about
singing live.

It started off with open auditions where anyone could
turn up. A friend of mine at Exeter University called Emily
Brett had seen an advert in one of the tabloids fronted by
Neil 'Dr' Fox. She cut it out and handed it to me in the
RAG office, which was the student union. I say it was the
student union but I never really knew what RAG did. I was
a member because Emily and I organised a charity fundraiser
called 'The Safer Sex Ball' – a big event where the whole of
the main campus was decorated for a huge party, essentially.
It raised at least £20,000 every year for the local HIV and
Aids charity, Positive Action South West. Everyone would
turn up in a 'sexy' outfit. I wore PVC red trousers from
Dorothy Perkins. (I still have them.) During *Pop Idol* the

headline would read 'WILL ORGANISED SEX PARTIES AT UNIVERSITY'. If only this was the case.

I rang the number on the newspaper clipping and got Neil Fox's cheery voice at the other end giving me the details. I left my name and number and then I think it was at this point I had to fill in a form that asked things like, 'Give five words to describe your character' (bubbly, curvaceous, fun-time girl, sporty); a bit about what you were doing in life (politics student who organises sex parties in his spare time); and who your idols were (Angela Bassett playing Tina Turner in the film *What's Love Got to Do with It?* I genuinely did put that one down). I think I might have used the word 'zany' to describe my sense of humour, which is just awful.

I posted off the form, then turned to my friend Adam and said: 'You know, I think I'm going to win this competition.'

That may all sound presumptuous, but the strange thing was that I had actually had a sort of premonition about a talent show that was looking for one singer. I remember being very frustrated in my final year at Exeter. I had such a desire to sing but I had no degree in singing, no recordings, I didn't play an instrument and I had no material of my own. I was aware I wasn't exactly marketable, being posh *and* gay. I wasn't cool. But I just had this feeling that if I could enter something that would get me directly in front of the public, then I would be all right. If I could bypass the music industry execs and just get to sing with a microphone on Saturday night TV, then I could make it.

I guess I had form, too. Two years previously, in my first year at university, I had entered a boy band competition on *This Morning*. *This Morning* is, of course, compulsory viewing for all good students. I had been watching it in my friend Fran's room when the competition was announced. Fran lived in the next-door halls of residence to mine and she had a television. This made her room a mecca.

Serena, who lived opposite Fran, was a very different type of person. More 'in control', you could say – extremely organised, clean and tidy. She was – and is – a very kind, wonderful person, but she would occasionally grow jealous of Fran's room being the centre of attention. One day she strode in and announced she also now had a television and, not only that, she had a bigger aerial than Fran's, so the reception was better. Her room was now officially open for 'televisual viewing', should anyone care to join her. She swept out of the room triumphantly.

There was a delay of ten minutes then Serena marched back in.

'Is no one coming to join me?' she asked.

We all looked at Serena as Fran proceeded to pull from under the bed a giant pack of pickled-onion Monster Munch, followed by a value pack of Haribo sweet and sours.

'Serena,' Fran said, popping a Haribo into her mouth with a satisfied air. 'These people ain't going anywhere.'

And so the war began.

Serena was also responsible for one of my favourite texts of all time, which simply stated: 'William, your washing powder is taking up valuable space in my room. Please come and collect NOW.'

She liked her room to be tidy.

So, anyway, Fran understood the almost mystical importance of snacks when it comes to serious TV watching. Any student will tell you that, along with a cheap bar, the most important amenity for any hall of residence is a snack shop, preferably within staggering distance of the cheap bar. Our snack provider was the local Esso garage, which was conveniently located at the bottom of the hill. It was the hub of all activity for our halls. Nights started and ended at the Esso garage. People got together and broke up at the Esso garage. New quantum theories were discussed over the Ginsters buffet bar at the Esso garage.

There was the famous Esso Cadbury's Creme Egg fight,

where the next day people went back to try to buy the security camera footage because it was so legendary. My friends Claire and Hugh almost broke up at the Esso, after Claire took Hugh for a smart birthday meal only for it to be regurgitated, along with Hugh's fake tooth, on the forecourt.

The Esso also played host to a moment that has become university folklore. For Esso really was the place where everyone went at the end of a night out. Because all the clubs and bars shut at the same time, and there wasn't a glowing array of venues to choose from, people would tend to descend on the Esso all at once. It was part of the night's routine, whether you were getting some noodles or more fags. On this particular night I had just turned up fresh from Samba Night at Time Piece. (Five quid for a jug of sangria was not to be sniffed at.) It was a Friday, a night when the student union was open, so most people were out – and as it was now about one-thirty in the morning, there was a sizable crowd at the Esso. The general mêlée was going on as usual when suddenly someone shouted: 'Look! Look across the road!'

We all looked and there, on the other side of the road, was a figure on the ground, slowly moving towards the garage.

'Oh my God,' someone else cried. 'It's Short Trousers Sophie!'

'Oh, yes,' a rather geeky bloke from Fran's corridor con- firmed. 'And she is sliding down the hill.'

'It looks like she's passed out.'

'Yeah,' the geeky guy agreed. 'But what is she sliding on?'

It was true: Short Trousers Sophie was sliding effortlessly on her front, arms placed neatly by her side, the backs of her hands scraping along the road. She resembled a Viking longboat rolling gracefully towards the sea.

I shouted out, 'I'll take a look!' and hopped across the road. As I neared Short Trousers Sophie, I let out a gasp of horror. 'Oh my goodness,' I said, to no one in particular. For Short Trousers Sophie had passed out but was still, in her unconscious state, heading towards Esso . . . sliding on her own vomit. I remember so clearly her grey cashmere trousers (short) and even the blue jumper she was wearing. Both were covered in sick. It was clear that she too had attended the Samba/Sangria Night from the colour of the vomit.

Years later I was to see Short Trousers Sophie in a pub, in fact just after I had done the first rounds of *Pop Idol*. She saw me and I saw her. Neither of us could bring ourselves to simply converse in pleasantries given what we both knew had happened that night, so we chose to ignore each other.

People still talk about the time that Short Trousers Sophie was carried on a stream of her own sick, slowly but surely towards the garage, clearly still intent on continuing the party with everyone else, even though she was passed out in a drunken stupor. She is something of a student legend.

So, back to Fran's room and the boy band announcement. We had just returned from the Esso garage with our morning supply of Quavers and fags and were settling down to watch *This Morning* when Richard and Judy announced the boy band competition. I thought, Right, a competition. This is a way of getting exposure on TV. I've got to go for it.

I dug out a picture that my dad had taken of me when I was seventeen, which was quite boy band-ish (vest, smouldering), and sent it off, along with a short description of myself and a recording of me singing 'Bridge Over Troubled Water'. I think there was just one round and then they contacted me to say that I had got through to the last ten and could come up to London to sing live on the show. The viewers would vote for their favourites and at the end of that morning four would be chosen to become *This Morning*'s boy band! It was very, very exciting.

On the day of the final I arrived early at the ITV studios on the South Bank, with nine other boys. I wore a woollen tank top, some wide black trousers and some new trainers. (The student loan was coming to good use!) We were cattled into the waiting room. There were no rehearsals. We were told we each had thirty seconds to sing a verse and a chorus in front of the judges. Before that we had to dance a little dance to Robbie Williams's 'Let Me Entertain You'.

There was a small stage with bright red curtains at the back and I remember being squeezed up behind them to give the illusion that there was lots of space behind the stage . . . which there wasn't. My name was called and out I sprang. It felt surreal to be on television for the first time. The stage really was tiny and there was a signpost on it saying 'Boy band auditions this way', which was a bit cringey. It was one of those out-of-body moments when I couldn't believe I was actually on television . . . and on *This Morning*, no less! It was exciting and terrifying.

The dance routine was embarrassing, the singing was okay. I sang the Jackson 5's 'I'll Be There'. My performance was being judged by Nigel Martin Smith of Take That fame, Kate Thornton, then editor of *Smash Hits*, and – guess who? – Simon Cowell!

We all waited around after our performances until the end of the show to hear the live results. The votes were counted and, lo and behold, I got in! The other three winners were Andy Scott Lee, whose sister Lisa was in Steps, a guy called Richard Knight (who I slightly fancied) and Lee Ryan, who went on to be in Blue.

I remember sitting down with Lee Ryan and him saying to me, think of all the girls we can shag! I concurred and said that I couldn't wait to shag all those girls. I had only come out two weeks previously so wasn't quite ready to be loud and proud.

So I won. I went to celebrate with my friend Camilla in McDonald's on the King's Road. Then I took the train back to Exeter and called my dad on the way, smoking a fag out of the window. (You were still allowed to do that then!) Dad said, 'Remember, William, you don't realise how important your anonymity is until you lose it. Do you really want to throw all your privacy away, potentially for the rest of your life?' What an auspicious conversation that was! He was very wise and right to ask me to think about that. Though it turned out my anonymity had nothing to worry about this time around.

At the time I didn't know what was going to happen with the boy band. We were expecting a recording contract. What was actually delivered was ... nothing. Well, I say nothing – there was the following week's 'make-over', where the new boy band went back to the studio for a restyle.

This Morning's boy band make-over lives in infamy among my mates.

'They are going to put you in chunky jewellery,' said my friend James.

'I reckon Acupunctures, definitely Acupunctures. Those moon-boot-like ones!' said Serena.

'Oh yeah, and some sort of bouffy blow-dried hair,' added Fran, nodding wisely.

'Ha, ha, very funny, guys. Of course they're not going to do that. It'll just be some sort of short-sleeved shirt and a fresh pair of jeans.'

'Mmm . . . you wait.' James mouthed 'moon boots' and began to step elaborately around the room like a spaceman while combing all of his hair down over his face.

'Fuck off.'

James was a great friend who was very well known at university for his success with the ladies and crazy antics. The ladies were often crazy themselves, prone to slashing tyres or cutting up ties when they were cast aside. James's greatest moment was when he dressed in full skiing gear, complete with skis and helmet, assumed the downhill position, and proceeded to ski down Longbrook Street, one of the main drags into town. I remember watching him cross the zebra crossing in front of the bus taking me to my 9 a.m. lecture.

James was, of course, spot on with his fashion predictions. I turned up to *This Morning* a week later and was confronted with a bevy of stylists, the three other guys from the band, and Nicky Clarke, who would be doing our hair for the make-over. I spied the Acupunctures and chunky jewellery laid out on a table, took a deep breath, and hoped that the ground would swallow me up. Either that or I could put on *all* the chunky jewellery and simply drown myself in the Thames before we went live. For I knew friends back in Exeter would be watching. And not just my friends, because since winning the competition I had become known as 'Boy Band Will'. I think I even went on university radio.

As the time came closer to reveal the new and improved *This Morning* boy band, Nicky Clarke was blow-drying my hair more and more. It was now huge and bouffy, just as Fran had predicted. I looked like one of the Beatles – just less hip and more monkey-like. And when I say 'monkey-like', I mean the band and the creature combined. Just as I was about to be revealed from behind yet another red curtain, Nicky Clarke looked at me and said, 'No, it hasn't worked, has it?'

My eyes widened and I was about to reply when—

Richard Madeley: 'And here's Will with *his* new look and... Oh, gosh, that is just... *great*? And I *love* the hair.'

I shuffled out from behind the curtain and looked at Richard. I wanted to punch him.

'You look great, Will.'

'No, I don't, Richard, you berk. I look like a complete

twat,' I said in my head. Out loud, I replied: 'Yes. Thank you.'

Nicky Clarke: 'Well, Richard, the hair just seemed to get bigger and bigger, didn't it, Will?'

'Yes, you fucking idiot, because you blow-dried it so much that it has practically taken over my entire face. Christ, I want to shave all of it off, wash myself, rip off all these clothes and run, run screaming out of this place towards the nearest noose.' What I actually said was: 'Yes, it just seemed to get bigger but I still LOVE it.'

Richard: 'And they've put you in some *great* Acupuncture shoes, which are very trendy, and some chunky jewellery.'

'Shoot me right now.' Actual reply: 'Yes.'

When I got out of the studio, I went for a drink with the other guys. I turned on my phone and listened to my voicemail. There was a message from everyone who had watched the show in Serena's room (who had clearly just bought a NASA satellite dish to lure people in). James was first. I couldn't actually hear what he was saying because he wasn't really saying anything – just panting with laughter. Finally, he managed to get two words out.

'Ch-er-unky jewellery,' he gasped.

Serena came on the phone next: 'MOON BOOTS!'

Then Fran: 'Bouffant hair!'

And then everyone fell apart laughing again. I hung up, put the phone in my pocket and turned to Lee.

'Was that your mates?'

'Yeah.'

'Bet they're jealous of your new look?'

'Oh, yeah. They're really jealous.'

I actually got quite upset after that. Not with my friends – they made fun of me about the make-over, but underneath all that they were supportive and proud. But I really thought I'd made it. We all thought we'd made it – we'd won! And then it came to nothing. There was no record contract. No band. It hurt to have my hopes and dreams dashed, but back I went to university and I just carried on with my studies (and threw away the ch-er-unky jewellery).

It was a lesson learned. Next time, I would not get so excited about a talent show.

Blame it on the Boogie

'. . . you know, I think I'm going to win this competition.'
I posted the *Pop Idol* form. 'I honestly just have that feeling.'

Not that I was getting overexcited.

A few days later a letter came back with my contestant
number and the date of my audition at the ExCeL Centre.
I got the DLR to the ExCeL, a place I had never heard of

before and am still confused as to what it is, incidentally. I officially opened the London Marathon there ten years later, and the MC introduced me as the man who had come second in *Popstars: The Rivals*. It was one of my proudest moments.

I turned up, registered and waited. And waited. And waited. My first round was with a lady called Claire. I walked into the room and sang Aretha Franklin's 'Until You Come Back to Me'. Claire's face was not moving and she didn't look convinced. I hit the bridge and her pen, which had been poised over the NO pile, moved across to the YES. I knew I had got her at that point.

'Yes,' she said.

And we were off.

There were two more rounds before you got to see the judges, and I think I had to return the next day because I'd changed my song by the time I got to that stage. My memory is hazy but I know I saw another lady called Camilla, who suggested that I should dance a bit more and sing something more upbeat. So the next day I came back with Michael Jackson (clearly a favourite of mine to audition with), 'Blame it on the Boogie'. This time I was seeing one of the producers, Ken. I sang for him and he put me through to the judges.

I was the last in line for the judges' audition. I sat waiting in a row of chairs, wearing some baggy jeans with a hole in the knee, my grandfather's old jumper (he had passed away recently and I wanted to carry his memory with me) and a vintage seventies football T-shirt underneath. Oh, and some old Doc Martens. The camera crew kept on wanting to talk to me and in the end I asked if they could leave me alone because I was trying to concentrate on the audition. Can you believe it? This might explain why there is very little footage of me before I reached the final fifty.

I sat in the corridor waiting to see these four people who I didn't know, but who held my fate in their hands. At that stage I didn't even know that Simon Cowell was one of the judges. The only one I knew would be there was Dr Fox.

I was waiting for quite simply the biggest audition of my life. Not the biggest moment. That, to date, had been coming out and I was sure there would be more moments to come – but in terms of my singing, this was huge. It was do or die time and I was more than aware of it. I felt sick but at the same time weirdly calm. It was like the feeling you get before a basketball game or an athletics meet – the adrenalin was pumping but I was completely focused. I tried to think positively and imagine how the audition was going to go and despite some terrifying thoughts, I had this real confidence that I would get through.

It's strange and comforting looking back – I can still remember that very deep, instinctive, ferocious belief that I was going to get through each round. Even when on the surface I had my fears and doubts, underneath it all, right at my core, there was a steely determination holding me together. And as soon as I stepped into that room it was a performance. With every inch of my body, from the shuffly walk to the coy smile and even the bad moves, I was giving out an energy that came from my soul that was saying, *You want me. You have to pick me.* It is so strange because I was so devoid of confidence in every other area of my life at that stage, but I just had this feeling – 100 per cent certainty – that I could do it. It is even weirder thinking about it because my audition really wasn't that good!

My name is called.

I walk into the room. It's massive. In front of me is a bank of bright lights, and behind them I can just make out a large crowd of people standing around watching me. (I find out later that, because I was the last contestant, every-one had filed in to see me.)

Shit. This is terrifying. What happened to all that confidence I had felt in the corridor? As my eyes travel round to the left I find the judges sitting at their table. My heart starts to pound. There's Pete Waterman, furthest away from the bank of lights. Then Nicki Chapman and Neil Fox in the middle. And then Simon Cowell at the other end... oh shit me, it's that man! I remember him from *This Morning*.

'William Robert Young,' Pete Waterman announces in a ponderous voice as I enter the room. 'You have come before this court today... and you are the last person we are gonna see in the whole series. What are you going to sing for us?'

I swallow hard. 'I'm going to sing "Blame it on the Boogie".'

'Okay, good luck,' Simon Cowell says.

I sing the song. I don't know why I chose it! Actually I do know why, I had a Michael Jackson mix tape in my car and it stood out as the best upbeat one to do. As I sing, I'm thinking, Oh dear, you'd better change the ending here, because it isn't going very well and you're singing, 'I just can't, I just can't, I just can't control my feet', which is ironic in itself because your leg keeps kicking out like a donkey's. I do the dance moves to the chorus. People do these dance moves at weddings.

'Sunshine.' (Point finger in air.)

'Moonlight.' (Spread hands.)

'Good times.' (Twitch involuntarily.)

'Boogie.' (Waggle legs in alarming fashion.)

I finish the song.

Pete Waterman speaks first but he doesn't really make much sense. He says he 'sort of liked it'. He has recorded that song three times with various artists and it is a song that haunts him. He likes my version. It's almost as if he's already preparing to leave the room, actually. His summary of my performance has left me none the wiser. I am now shaking with nerves.

Nicki Chapman speaks next. She liked my singing voice. She did not like my moves *at all*. Overall, though, she enjoyed it. She isn't giving the game away, either.

Fuuuck! Oh, fuck. This isn't exactly ground-breakingly positive.

Foxy's next. Foxy. What a cheery, positive bundle of energy! Even his name denotes fun and frolics. He found it cheesy. He then goes on for a minute about what kind of cheese it was. I like this man. His response is the most positive, a pleasant cheese, he says.

Right, one in the bag . . . I think.

Finally, Simon Cowell says he thought it was okay and

then asks for all of the others to say whether I am through or not.

Waterman: 'You turn up in scrappy trousers, an old jumper with stains on it and boots that haven't seen any polish and you expect me to put you through? No way, kid. It's a no from me.'

Fuck, he's changed his tune, hasn't he, the old codger? His lip is curling and everything. And, incidentally, it is my grandfather's jumper, so I couldn't give a shit if you don't like it. *I* do.

Chapman: 'It's a yes from me.'

YEEESSSS! I like this lady. I like her a lot!

Foxy: 'I like you. It's a yes from me, too.'

YEEEEEEESSSSSSS! This is good! Foxy, you bloody brilliant man!

Cowell: 'I have the deciding vote. I am head of the judges, so it is up to me if you go through or not.'

Oh, bollocks.

'You're a good-looking boy...'

Oh God, I think I'm going to be sick.

'... You've got a nice voice...'

Thank you...

'... Does it mean a lot to you?'

Pause.

What? Why is this man asking me that? Is this the point when I say '*this much*', and slowly drop to my knees? I mean, the cameras are rolling, but a quick favour under the judges' desk might be all it takes to get through. I opt for a simple, spoken reply and a completely earnest one.

'Yes. Yes it does.'

'Well then, you are through to the next round. Congratulations.'

OH MY GOD! OH MY GOD! I got through. I GOT THROUGH! I can't believe it. I feel so happy. This is *amazing*! I walk back into the corridor and then outside for a cigarette on the balcony, which runs alongside the judging room. One of the girls who had put me through an earlier round comes up as everyone is loading stuff away and says, 'Everyone was rooting for you.'

Really? 'Thank you.' I still can't believe it.

'Good luck for Boot Camp. Here's your pack with all the info. See you in a few weeks.'

'Thank you,' I say again, stunned.

I had a few weeks between getting through that first judges' audition and the start of Boot Camp in September. (It wasn't actually called Boot Camp back then, but that's effectively what it was.) The information pack included details of what we would be doing for those next few days of auditions, which would whittle us down to the final fifty.

My memory is hazy as to what order it went in, but I know that for the boys we had to sing two songs. The choices in one group were between Robbie Williams's 'Let Me Entertain You' (again!) or George Michael's 'Fast Love'. The other song everyone had to sing was the Drifters' 'Up on the Roof'. I had to buy a copy of *The Best of the Drifters* so I could learn it, which is funny because now you could just go on YouTube, of course, but back then I had to go and get the CD from a record store. How archaic! Also, it was expensive! I was working as a gardener and holding down two waiting jobs at the time.

While I was prepping for the next round of *Pop Idol* auditions, work still had to be done to pay for the train fares or petrol to London. I would work during the day and rehearse my chosen songs in the evening. I always liked to practise in a space with good acoustics and I was still shy about my singing, so I used to go down the road to a tiny old church where I had once attended nursery school. It has since been renovated into a house, but back then it was quiet, if a bit dilapidated. I would sneak in to practise the Drifters song or George Michael. 'Fast Love' was actually a very hard song to sing. It wasn't something you could really get your teeth into. I was worried about singing it, but I really had no choice because the other option was 'Let Me Entertain You', and Robbie Williams songs are so much about him and his performance, and it's impossible to recreate that. I was thankful for the Drifters song.

Time passed and at last it was September and time for Boot Camp, which took place at the Criterion Theatre on Piccadilly Circus. I got to the theatre and waited to be brought out on stage with everyone else. It was frightening beyond belief. Everyone seemed so confident, with big personalities, singing out loud and wearing glamorous clothes. I sat in a corner with my woolly hat on and went into myself.

I was very used to doing that. I would often withdraw from situations, imagine going into my body and creating a protective layer around myself. I wouldn't speak to anyone. I discovered in later years that people sometimes mistook this for rudeness, but in fact I was just painfully shy. I wanted to make myself as inoffensive as possible so I would speak very quietly and avoid any eye contact. It was a survival mechanism. In any new situation I was always more of a watcher than someone who jumped in both feet first. I did this at every school when I first joined, including my drama school and university. I preferred to start quiet.

We were all called up onto the stage and told that we would be getting cut twice to get down to the final fifty. The first audition was to be the Drifters song, which would be sung in groups of three. We were assigned to our groups and told to sort out among ourselves who was going to sing which bit. We stood in a simple triangle and came to the front when it was our turn to perform a solo.

Performance over, we waited for the results. While waiting, I noticed that the cameras were very focused on a young pretty boy in a denim suit with spiky hair. There was obviously some sort of buzz around him, so I listened in to his interview. He had a stutter. A very heavy one. He could hardly get a word out. Poor chap.

Everyone was noticing him now, and I could feel the jealousy in the room about the attention he was receiving. Well, he is obviously going to get through, I thought. It was like watching someone who was already a celebrity.

'I bet it's all made up,' said a girl next to me.

'What, the stutter?'

'Yes.' She frowned over at the boy.

'Well, if it is,' I said, 'he is one clever bastard.'

When the judges were ready for us, we were called back onto the stage in different lines and told whether we had got through. This was beginning to mean more to me than I had thought it would or wanted to admit. I was getting closer to being on live TV and, more importantly, closer to letting the public decide my fate. But the songs I was being asked to sing made me feel so restricted – I just couldn't get out what I really wanted to. If I could just sing a song of my choice, I knew everything would change.

With all of this in mind, I suddenly realised that I wanted to get through so badly . . . and that I would be devastated if I didn't. Shit.

We all lined up.

There was a long pause . . . then: 'You are all through to the next round!'

Yeeeeeeeesssssssssss! I jumped around and even hugged someone I didn't know, which was unlike me. We all ran to the downstairs bar and milled around excitedly. I went up to the bar to get a glass of water and saw that the barman was ashen-faced. I was on such a high, I couldn't understand it.

'What's happened?' I asked.

'It's awful,' he said. 'A plane has flown into the Twin Towers in New York.'

I thought I was watching a movie. I turned on the television in my hotel room on Tottenham Court Road to watch a plane flying into a building. It knocked me back on to the bed. This was real life, this wasn't a film. I could see the text running along the bottom of the screen that showed it was twenty-four-hour news. I couldn't believe it.

I knew that I had at least four hours to wait before I discovered if I was through to the final fifty. I walked out of my room, out of the hotel, and jumped on a tube to my friend Mary's flat – I was starting a three-year course at ArtsEd (short for Arts Educational Schools) in Chiswick the following week and I'd just moved in. (Little did I know that within a year I would be scrubbing the flat's newly laid front steps due to people writing 'I Love You Will' on them.)

When I got to Ladbroke Grove I met Mary for a coffee. The feeling in London was intense and palpable. Everything felt slower. I felt more connected to people – complete strangers – and at the same time had a sudden urge to be connected with friends. All my thoughts about whether I had got through or not had been put into perspective.

The afternoon's auditions had passed without a hitch. I'd sung 'Fast Love' and thought it had gone well. It was a bitch of a song to sing. Now I had to wait, but I had a different outlook on the whole show. If I got through then great. If I didn't then, look, life is so precious, I had my health and I was alive. The rest was a bonus.

I headed back to the hotel where everyone was staying and waited upstairs with the rest for our results. The cameras were zooming around and I did my best to stay out of the way. There was one point when I couldn't hide from the camera or hide my feelings. There was a comeback in motion during these auditions. A comeback that involved someone who had already been in the talent show *Popstars*, and although he was seen as a bit of a laughing stock, he had returned for a second pop. He had shorter hair this time, but he still had the guitar. Darius Danesh. Everyone was very excited to see Darius – he was a real-life celebrity. I was not among these people. Unfortunately, I found myself squashed up on the end of a sofa with him perched on the arm, strumming his guitar and singing. The film crew could not miss such an opportunity and recorded this moment for posterity. The camera starts at one end of the sofa and pans along, with everyone staring adoringly towards Darius... until it hits my face. I couldn't look any more disgusted! The last thing I needed before finding out what was going to happen in my life was Darius Danesh singing an earnestly rendered 'Papa Don't Preach' in my ear.

With Darius's mini-concert over, our names were called out and we were sent into one of several different rooms. We had no idea how many rooms there were, and so no idea how many different groups could go through to make up the fifty.

I walked into my allocated room and looking around could see there weren't many people in there. Uh-oh, this was not a good sign, not a good sign at all. What was worse was *Darius* was in there with me. I tell you, if he started singing now... Well, actually, I stopped to think about this. Surely they would have to put Darius through? I mean, he was TV gold, wasn't he? Or maybe it meant they were really clamping down on any hint of a novelty act? In which case Darius was going... and so was I.

While I was trying to work this out, we heard a massive cheer from one of the next-door rooms. SHIT. Okay, so that was a very big room by the sound of the cheers, which meant that we were obviously in the No Room. My shoulders slumped and my head fell. Defeat had arrived and while I knew it wasn't the end of the world, it was hard to take. I had come such a long way but now it was over. At least I started college on the Monday where a whole new world would open up before me. It just wasn't the one that I'd dreamed of.

The doors opened and in walked the judges. Simon Cowell spoke.

'You guys are in the Maybe Room. It was a really close decision and I'm afraid . . .'

I couldn't even look up. Couldn't even breathe.

'. . . I'm afraid you are all through!'

Silence in my head. White noise.

Then a raging waterfall and a dozen choirs!

WHAT?

I jumped, I leaped around, I think I even hugged Darius. Oh, hang on, I didn't do that. I did hug Foxy, however.

This was just the best news. I couldn't believe it. I COULDN'T BELIEVE IT! I mean, this was happening now. NOW IT WAS HAPPENING! I am going to sing on a proper microphone, with a nice echo, and I don't have to rely on judges but I can sing directly to the public! Shit me.

I reconnected with that belief, that moment when I

turned to Adam as I posted the letter and said, 'I think I can win this.'

You know what, I thought, I think I might just bloody do it!

Let battle commence

'I think we should make a programme called *Waiter Watch*.'

'I don't *watch* him, William.'

'Oh, really.'

'No,' Michael says, sighing gently as he flicks through *Grazia*, eyes still firmly fixed on the waiter. 'No, I suggest to him. I coax. I tease. I . . . propose. I don't *watch*.'

'Right.'

He turns the page, points to a photograph of Simon Cowell at some charity ball. 'You know, he is kind of hot, Simon Cowell.'

'Oh, Michael . . . really? You really think Simon Cowell is hot?'

'Yes. Yes I do.'

Michael has bleached his hair. It sort of suits him. He is wearing a really quite small, tight T-shirt underneath a rough denim waistcoat and his little tummy is sticking out. Somehow, he is managing to make the whole outfit work, even though it really shouldn't. He circulates his spoon slowly around his green tea.

'I mean, think about it. The man wears black. The *whole* time. He has a good frame, he is funny, intelligent and, most importantly, *loads of cash!*'

I pull a face. 'I am *actually* halfway through my croissant and I do want to *actually* finish it, please.'

'I'm just saying, rather than answering back, you should have made your move . . . Oh, hold up – here he comes.'

The waiter approaches, gives me another coffee and hands Michael a muffin with a little smile.

'Thank you. Thank you so much. Very kind.'

The waiter goes.

'Ha! Did you see that? I knew it! You saw the smile, didn't you? Oh yes . . . here we go.'

'He *did* smile,' I acknowledge.

'Yes, he smiled all right. I am going to leave my number.'

'Engraved in that muffin?'

'Ha – very funny. It's just a matter of time.' He shifts in his chair and narrows his eyes at the waiter.

'What happened to Cowell?' I ask.

'Oh, you can have him.' He shrugs. 'And you should write about that whole "talking back" moment.' He leans back and pops a piece of muffin into his mouth. 'Let's be honest, it was the only thing that made you remotely interesting.'

'You are a really good friend, Michael.'

Michael sighs. 'I know, William, I know. To a fault.'

Life was very rushed between finding out I had got into the final fifty, hugging Neil Fox and starting college at ArtsEd. Oh, and basically moving up to London. I settled into living in Ladbroke Grove. The flat was next door to the house where Jimi Hendrix had died. American tourists would often wander over from Portobello Market to take pictures. One sunny morning after my first week at ArtsEd, I was leaning out of the window, drinking my coffee and smoking a fag. The Americans soon started arriving and taking their holiday snaps. I had newly acquired a toy cat that was extremely life-like and used to purr, lift up its tail and even hiss. As the Americans were looking up I reached for the cat and brought it out onto the window ledge. The tourists went nuts, pointing and cooing and taking even more photos. I started stroking the cat. More photos and oohs and aaahhs. Then I grabbed the cat by its tail and started slamming its face against the outer wall of the building. Everyone went crazy.

'Oh my God, Gerald, GERALD, look what he's doing to that poor cat!'

'Quick, call 911!'

Chuckling away now, I placed the cat's head under the window and proceeded to slam the window up and down like a guillotine.

'Oh, *Jesus!*' cried a really fat tourist. 'This is just AWFUL! Eugene, you take some pictures of this awful, awful bad boy. You hear me? YOU'RE AN AWFUL BAD BOY YOU ARE, AND WE ARE CALLING THE POLICE!'

This became a regular thing that I would do to scare the tourists. I know it was naughty, but the sound of their chattering first thing on a Saturday morning was just too tempting!

Every morning I would get up around seven, get ready and set off for Turnham Green, where ArtsEd was based. The school was strict on punctuality. It had a rule – three strikes and you were out. I think by half term I was already on two. How long I would have lasted there if I hadn't continued in the competition is probably up for debate.

ArtsEd was a completely new experience for me. The first day we all had to get up and introduce ourselves. I told no one of my success in *Pop Idol* to that point. I preferred to keep it secret. There was another boy who was in the competition who it is not unfair to say was definitely *not* quiet about his involvement. He too had got through to the final fifty. He was a strong contender and a bit of a golden boy at ArtsEd. I decided to keep my involvement less public and just get on with daily school life.

There was a lot to do – ballet, tap, Alexander technique, voice work, acting, jazz and contemporary dance, Pilates, singing lessons with two different teachers. It was like being in the army. But in Lycra. It was a far cry from writing essays on Marxism at Exeter.

I had A levels and a Politics degree, but I hadn't taken a single acting, singing or dancing lesson in my life. Also, at twenty-two, I was one of the oldest students in the whole school, even though I was in the first year! As I wandered down the long halls of ArtsEd in my baggy jeans and my uncle's vintage *Sgt Pepper* coat, the boys would jeté and pirouette past me in their tight black onesies. I *hated* wearing the tight black tights we were made to wear for ballet in particular and would always pretend I had forgotten them. (God, it only took me ten years – in my video for 'Jealousy' I wore tight *white* Lycra! I got there in the end!)

I felt so conscious of my body and I didn't want anyone to know whether I was gay or straight. I had come out at Exeter, but these were new people and I didn't like the idea of being put into a box and judged by them. I was extremely prudish about it and this was cause for chatter in the student bar and, of course, the boys' changing room. I remember walking in there and being amazed by the number of boys applying make-up in front of the mirror. I then opened my locker and there was a note that simply said, 'I think you are really cute'. I shut the door quickly. Who wrote it? I was terrified and a little bit excited at the same time. I looked around but caught no one's eye.

On the Friday evening of my first week we all went for a drink in the student bar and a girl just marched up to me and said, 'We all want to know, are you gay or straight?'

'I don't know if that is anyone's business,' was my rather uppity reply. Then I paused, thought about it and said, 'But, for the record, I am gay.'

The girl went back to her group of second years. 'Told you,' I heard her say.

I had a very stern approach to my sexuality back then. I hated the idea of people judging me and putting me into a box because they found out I was gay. The beginnings of me saying out loud that I was gay were the beginnings of me opening up about my sexuality more generally, and I started to get the chance to act on this, which I hadn't at university.

Essentially, what I'm saying is that I finally managed to get a shag!

Being at ArtsEd was exactly like being in *Fame!*, and I have to say I relished it in many ways. I relished the discipline. I relished the hard work. I was finally able to study and work hard at stuff I had wanted to do for years. Things were coming together. I had gone to ArtsEd not out of a love for musical theatre but out of a feeling that I had to get some physical, technical training to allow me to then go into the world of 'pop'. This was something I believed very strongly. I couldn't just walk into a drinks party in London and say, 'Oh, hi, I want to be a singer' when people asked what I wanted to do. I felt that I needed some kind of springboard.

I don't think I would have lasted the three years. Musicals weren't for me at the time. I couldn't get on in my singing lessons and I knew there was an important part of my voice that would be lost on musical theatre. Also, I don't think I could have afforded it. My grandmother lent me some money for the first year that I would have run out of. I had a job at a pub but the ArtsEd workload was so heavy during term time that I couldn't work during the week. I wouldn't have been able to afford to stay there for the three years.

As a starting point and experience, though, I loved it. I remember turning up to dance lessons on a Monday morning – jazz with Jackie Bristo (which was an institution in itself) – and we would all practise our pirouettes. I would be falling all over the place, cursing myself, looking like an idiot, while the trains whizzed by right outside the window and I would think, God, this is bloody great. I have wanted to do this for such a long time. I was dedicated. I would stay after school with my friends Scott and Laura and we would practise our turns and our ballet until quite late. My God, it really was *Fame!*

Our set was seen as the joke set for there was a great deal of rivalry within the college and within our year. My set was made up of all the odds and sods: we had tall and thin, fat and short, every race and creed, and every type of character. We also had a laugh! Often people from the top set would saunter past our hapless ballet class with their noses up in the air and it used to spur us on.

We were screamed and shouted at by all the teachers, particularly in dance.

'Michael, you big useless lump, get your effing feet off the ground.'

'Oh, Natalie, stop dawdling around like an insect and at least *try* to do it properly.'

'William, are you a man or are you a fairy, because you can't seem to make up your mind?'

They were horrible to us, but it didn't matter. It toughened us up, and it is a tough business. We were rarely, if ever, praised. Particularly in Jackie's class. But she was also the kindest of the lot. She knew how much it meant to us. She had been there herself. It was a front. In she would come and the screaming would begin. In a funny way, I enjoyed it. Sometimes I would sit there while attempting the splits, with Jackie running her nails up my back saying, 'Will this back *ever* get straight, William? I mean, *will* it?' And I would be pouring sweat onto the floor, thinking, William, you are twenty-two. You've got a Politics degree.

(Okay, it's a 2:2 but it's still a degree.) You were offered a job at Sony Publishing. You could be working in the City. Instead you are sitting here in Lycra, a very tight vest and a headband and you are attempting to do something that quite frankly you will never achieve. The splits.'

Then my other voice would say, Oh, but come on, your arse looks amazing in these leggings and you and everyone else knows it.

Argument won.

I loved the physicality of the classes, actually. Not since playing rugby at school had I really worked so hard with my body and I was enjoying it and slowly learning to enjoy my new-found physique.

Of all the students in my set, I remember Colin in particular. He was from Bolton; he was tall and strawberry blond; he was living with a much older guy, which seemed *so* exotic; and he enjoyed dressing up as a lady. He was also one of the funniest guys I have ever met. There was something untouchable about him, which I think there often is with transvestites. They occupy a very specific space, and I think as a man just having the balls (pardon the phrase) to walk out wearing a dress immediately gives off a fantastic fuck-you attitude.

Our ballet teacher David was fond of Colin, too, but he

would still scream at him: 'Colin, will you ever get that arse actually in the air?'

To which Colin would drawl back: 'Depends what time of day it is, David.'

We would roll around laughing, and even David would crack a smile. The thing about Colin was that he didn't have a bad bone in his body and he was confident in who he was, so he commanded respect. I think a lot of our set were very individual and I hope that the people I spent that one short term with have retained that individuality because it was what made them and made us as a class.

During this first term of pirouettes and Lycra, sexual awakening and corridors of *Fame!*, I was slowly heading towards true fame. For, during half term, I would be appearing in one of the five initial rounds that would determine whether I would become one of the final ten contenders performing on live Saturday night TV.

As a reminder: we had got down to fifty contestants. Each week, ten of us would sing in front of the judges and then people would phone in live on the night the show was aired and the results would be read out at 10 p.m. on Saturday night. Only two contestants each week would go through to the live finals. The performance itself was not screened live at that stage but filmed midweek, which made it even worse because you had to wait from Wednesday evening to Saturday night to find out if the public liked you enough to send you through to the next round.

I was in the fourth of the five heats, competing with nine other singers. When my week came around, I set off for Fountain Studios, the TV studios where the show was filmed, feeling both excited and apprehensive. ArtsEd had prepared me even in just a few weeks to feel a bit more professional and this was my mantra: 'Be professional and polite and get the job done!'

The ten of us were staying in a Travelodge near Kew Gardens and we all got on well. I particularly remember a lovely girl called Becky who was really pretty, but unfortunately had very little confidence. For two days we rehearsed at the studios, spoke to the press, did some filming for the ITV2 behind-the-scenes show, and practised with our vocal coaches David and Carrie Grant, with Mike Dixon accompanying us on the piano. Kate Thornton was fronting the ITV2 show. (Ant and Dec presented the main ITV programme.) This was the same Kate Thornton who had been a judge on the *This Morning* boy band competition. Small frigging world, isn't it? We got on well from the beginning and she was an ally.

Korben was another contestant in our group. (His real

name is Chris Niblet, which always makes me chuckle.) He was a good singer, and far more confident than me. He was also another 'gay' – and two gays in one room can be like releasing two tom-cats into a ring. A lot of hissing. We had different approaches, though – he was loud and confident, I was quiet and stealthy!

Looking back, what was so great about those few days was that we were all such different people. There was another guy called Craig Thomas, who was sweet, and a young, very pretty girl called Nathalie. Sally Goodison was loud, brassy and great fun. We all got thrown together. I would be lying if I said I wasn't sitting there weighing up if I thought I was better than the others or not. It was a competition after all, and I wanted to get through.

I did have a belief in what I was rehearsing and I was comforted and encouraged by the way David, Carrie and Mike reacted to my singing. We had been asked to come along with two song options. My first was Elton John's 'I'm Still Standing' and my second was the Doors' 'Light My Fire'. I had done some initial practice at college, but not much. When I started singing 'Light My Fire' at Fountain Studios, the whole vocal team said this was the one I had to do and even though they were meant to be impartial I could see they were excited.

This was compounded further when Mike Dixon caught up with me on the Tuesday and offered me a chance to audition for a brand-new musical he was working on called *We Will Rock You*. Even at that stage I felt I had hit the jackpot. I remember thinking, Well, that's it! I am studying at ArtsEd to get the chance to leave and be offered roles on the West End stage and now someone has just offered me a chance to walk straight into an audition after less than half a term of training! It gave me such a boost of confidence. After years of having a secret belief in my singing, someone had just given me a huge rush by saying he believed in my ability too, enough to offer me a chance to be in a new musical.

It helped calm my nerves, because I now knew that even if I didn't get through, I wouldn't go back to ArtsEd. I already felt that it wasn't going to be my home. I was getting a taste and a sense of what I really wanted – and what could be in store for me.

Along with these first inklings of self-belief, there was conflict brewing between me and Simon Cowell. Of course, in the ten years since I met him, Simon has become very famous. In terms of career trajectories, his has gone stratospheric. People still ask me about him. 'Do you see him?' 'Does he have anything to do with your music?' 'Do you like him?' He holds such fascination for people and I can understand why. *I'm* fascinated by him! My God... maybe I fancy him? (I don't fancy him.)

When it came to the week of my 'heats', I already knew I was heading towards a confrontation one way or another. Not only had I experienced my own brief brushes with him but I had watched the three rounds of the show before mine and I had seen the way he was dispatching the various contestants. He was gaining a reputation for himself. People were talking about the 'nasty judge' and the ratings for the show were climbing week by week. But in the process, he destroyed people. Quite simply, he crushed people's dreams. It made for dramatic TV and kept the public gripped. But it was also incredibly tough on the contestants, and like many people I thought some of his comments were mean-spirited.

Watching it week in, week out, I was aware that I was going to have to step into the ring with this man. It's weird but I knew what he was going to try to do. I knew he would try to take me down. I don't know how I knew, I just did. With that in mind, I watched the third show with my father. He turned to me after it had finished and Cowell had shredded a few more people's confidence and self-esteem, and he said, 'William, I have not brought you

up to be bullied by people like that. If he tries to bully you, then you stand up for yourself. That man is a coward.'

The battle was going to commence and I was prepared for it. What happened next was one of the defining moments in my life.

'. . . and we introduce you, you walk out of the green room and then you stop. We then move the cameras around, you restart your walk and you stop at the microphone stand. You then wait again, we reset the cameras and you then start the song.'

'Okay,' I reply to the floor manager. Christ. Talk about trying to remain focused. Welcome to the world of TV.

'Coming to you "as live" in three, two, one . . . and GO, Dec! GO, Ant!'

'Right, Will, you are up next. Good luck and off you go.'

Shit! This is it. Judgement Day. I've got to go out there and face these almost mythical people again. Last time I saw them was in a holding room, the Maybe Room to be precise, at the hotel in London. They have an air about them. They are so important to my career, even though it has moved to public vote. I am wearing Miu Miu trousers my mum bought me from Harvey Nichols and a dark brown Zara shirt I managed to blag from the shop. Me and my flatmate Mary, who is a stylist, rang up the head office, told them I was coming on the show, and in I went to the main store on Oxford Street. And they said I could take anything I wanted. Amazing! Mary was great because I just kept on grabbing more and more cardigans whereas she stressed I *actually* needed to get something I could wear for the performance.

As I walk out and go through the rigmarole of stopping and reshooting my walk to the microphone, I have gone calm. I feel like I am untouchable. I am suddenly not scared. I think of the times when I was down at university, I think of my grandfather and of a close family friend who recently passed away from a brain tumour, and I think, This is nothing in the grand scheme of things. Yes, it is important and it could bring me all my dreams, but it also needs to be put in perspective. These judges cannot harm me. What they say will not alter how I feel about my ability. So all I have to do now is give a performance that I'm proud of and that people I hold dear will hopefully be proud of.

'Hello.'

'Hello, how are you?' says Nicki Chapman.

'Very well, thanks. How are you?' Christ, William, this is no time for pleasantries, get on and sing the fucking song. I do like her, though. Foxy is smiling. Pete Waterman seems a tad vacant. Simon already looks bored.

And we are off. Think about the breathing, William. Think about the tone, enjoy the tone down low. Now, when you go up the octave, enjoy the change, hit it with an explosion. Surprise them. Yes, this is going well. Fuck, I am enjoying this. Me and a microphone and the cameras. *Yes!* Don't forget to look at the cameras. Smile.

And we are done. Song finished. You didn't forget your words and you haven't fainted.

Wait, camera reset, and . . . turn to judges.

Nicki . . . she really liked it.

Foxy . . . he really liked it.

Waterman . . . he says I woke him up and he thanks me for that. Does this man ever speak non-cryptically?

Cowell. And here we go.

'It is a bit like you singing around your family table at Sunday lunch.'

I am mute. I have to say something. My mouth won't open. Shit. Come on, William, this is your time, don't let this guy shout you down. I can't though. I can't find the breath or the words. Then a voice pipes up.

'Please don't take that. Please say something back.'

It's Nicki. She wants me to say something. She gives me the nudge I need and suddenly I find the words, I find the breath and I speak. And as I am speaking, I know he is going to try to interrupt me, but I've got that one covered.

'Sorry,' I interject. 'Can I finish speaking, please?' Yes, three years of Politics tutorials were not completely wasted. He is on the back foot. It all comes out. I am polite, eloquent, and then I say some words I never felt I could say out loud about my performance.

'I don't think you could ever call that average.'

I can't believe it. I can't believe I have so brazenly said that my performance was good. My God, isn't that so arrogant? So cocky? Yet it doesn't feel cocky. It just feels like the truth. Something has come out of me that I never thought ever would, a public declaration that I actually feel I am good and talented.

Simon calls me a gentleman. I thank him and then wait for the cameras to reset. So I have to stand on the stage for about a minute after this epic exchange of words, just waiting there in silence. It is actually fucking funny. Part of me wants to bring up something really trivial – like the weather or their journeys to the studio. I think about mentioning train journeys, but I know that might set Pete off, being a train enthusiast.

'Okay, if we could just have the end again, Will . . .'

'Thank you,' I say again and turn and walk out. And as I walk out I think, William, you may have just changed your life in that moment.

And the truth is . . . I did.

We finished the show and I gave an interview saying my dad would say, 'You're not taking that, my boy,' and that he would say to my mum, 'Annabel, get the shotgun!', which I think people still to this day say to my dad around our home town.

I waited for three days, then Saturday came around and it was time for the live results. I went with a friend, Katie. The show aired, I got through along with Chris Niblet – sorry, I mean Korben – and off I went to a club in Clapham where thirty or forty friends were waiting and we all got absolutely shit-faced. I ended the night in the kebab shop round the corner and woke up the next morning as 'the guy who answered back'.

The following Monday I started back at ArtsEd for the second half of the term. After the initial excitement and a mention at the morning assembly, it was all back to normal. I got on with what I had to do, which was more ballet, Lycra, acting classes, tap, etc. Colin continued to have our class in stitches, there was the odd fumble for me sexually, and suddenly I had finished the Christmas term.

The following week I was into the final ten of *Pop Idol*. From then it was a countdown, with the person with the least votes disappearing every week, until there were just two in the final and an eventual winner.

Week One

I wear a check tank top and surf jeans with white stitching. My hair is slicked down at the front but teased up at the back. I look like I am wearing a chessboard, with weird Worzel Gummidge hair. I am also singing Aretha Franklin. Quite how people could even suspect me of being straight is beyond me. I might as well hold up a sign saying, 'I am gay!' Rick Waller, who is very large, is off ill with a bad throat. I sing well and Cowell apologises.

Week Two

Rick Waller pulls out of the show. And guess who makes a reappearance? Only bloody Darius Danesh! Christ, talk about the cat with nine lives. He is the one to watch. I sing 'Winter Wonderland' in a see-through shirt. If the Aretha Franklin song wasn't enough of a beacon, surely the shirt will alert the non-believers? There is a big Christmas tree on stage with us. Rosie Ribbons gives a performance of 'Santa Baby' that probably should be screened post-watershed.

Week Three

Burt Bacharach week. 'Wives and Lovers' is my song choice. I wear a red velvet suit with faint pinstripes. Darius is playing it well, Hayley shines, Gareth is favourite. Nicki Chapman likes me. Cowell likes Gareth.

Week Four

Film week. I sing 'Ain't No Sunshine'. It is my breakthrough moment. Great performance. I wear an Aertex leather jacket. Things are looking up in the style stakes.

Nicki pays me a compliment – 'I don't think you are getting big headed.' She is a very clever woman. She doesn't
want me to peak too soon and for people to turn against
me. I like her. I like her a lot. She also says I would be a
welcome addition to the 19 stable – Simon Fuller's management company, which is backing the show. My
grandmother rings me afterwards and asks why I am
going to a stable. I am equally confused. Pete Waterman
says I have one of the best recording voices he has heard
in twenty years. Suddenly I have really warmed to this
man.

Week Five

The behemoth that is ABBA week! I wear my dad's old
suede flares. Darius is still going strong. Christ, how does
he do it? Gareth untouchable. Zoe looking good. We have
lost Korben, Aaron, Laura and Jessica Garlick. Rosie gives
a dreadful performance of 'The Winner Takes It All'. Her
voice clicks out of key and she can never get back in tune
after that. She knows it and off she goes. Pete Waterman is
in a big sulk about the whole week. Everyone is in a sulk –
judges, production team. We poor contestants are stuck in
the middle, so we all drink ourselves into oblivion after the

show. Viewing figures are growing rapidly, press coverage is building. The show is becoming a runaway smash hit and nerves are jangling all around us.

Week Six

Big band week and my birthday! We all go to Soho House afterwards and have a party – God, it's fun. We basically have an excuse for a party every Saturday night. My friends have taken Fountain Studios by storm and befriended most of the production team. I wear my grandfather's cufflinks and my grandmother is in the audience. (Damn it – I gave the security guards pictures and *told* them not to let her in.) Hayley goes, despite giving the most mesmerising performance of 'That Ole Devil Called Love'. She has a great voice and we got on well. We smoked and gossiped and shared worries. She's a lovely down-to-earth girl and she will be missed.

Week Seven

Number ones week. Not my favourite or my best. I sing the Eurythmics' 'There Must Be an Angel' and the Bee Gees' 'Night Fever'. It's all a bit karaoke but I scrape through. Zoe goes despite Darius singing on a chair, then standing up. Life can be cruel. It's me, Darius and Gareth in the final three. I'm damned if I'm being kicked out by Darius.

Week Eight

Songs decided by the judges. I get 'Sweetest Feeling' and 'Beyond the Sea'. They are very good choices and they get me into the final. Home stretch now.

Week Nine

'Battle buses'. What a week. Gareth and I are given our own tour buses and shipped round the country to do publicity and rally our fans. I've done every show under the sun and have even met Helena Bonham Carter (amazing!). Now here we are back at Fountain Studios for the final. Twelve and a half million people will watch this show. I almost have a meltdown in dress rehearsal because the fucking songs are so hard to sing, especially 'Anything Is Bloody Possible'. The judges watch the dress rehearsal and it is clear from the looks on their faces that they think Gareth is going to get it. My rehearsal is awful. Annie Lennox drops by my dressing room and says her advice is 'Fuck 'em!' Shit me, I love that woman. My mum comes in next. She is excited about seeing Annie Lennox too! I feel a bit like I might at my own wedding, I suppose. Everyone has a part to play: the mother of the boy in the final; the best friend of the boy in the final; the grandmother of... God, did she get in *again*? I sing 'Light My Fire' and spot Annie Lennox singing along in the audience. I could go home happy at that point. The results come in. Long, LONG pause from Ant and Dec.

And the winner is...

WILL!

It's me? IT'S ME! Fucking hell! FUCKING HELL!

FUUUCCCKKKIIIIINNNNGGGG HEEELLLLL-LLL!

I've only gone and bloody done it!

Hug Gareth. Go and sing winner's song. Someone puts the lyrics on autocue, thank God. Confetti gets in my mouth. Darius is there, lifting me up. Oh Darius, get OFF. Finish song, interview, hug family. Uncle Jeremy is in the corridor – so, so proud. My mum is dancing with Foxy – disturbing. My grandmother is overwhelmed but content. It has given her a new lease of life after Grandad dying – emotional and wonderful. My friends – shit-faced. It's as if they have all decided to get off with each other after years of being just friends. Dance dance dance, lots of pictures, lots of smiles and back to the hotel. Friends are continuing to cop off with each other. The sun comes up.

PAUSE!

In bed, I think to myself with a nervous smile:

I only went and bloody won the effing thing.

Wow . . .

Sleep.

'This looks like a man who won't say no to a sausage'

It was my friend Steph's summer party at her parents' house outside Reading. We had just finished our first year at university and a load of us were in the garden to celebrate our summer holidays.

I lined up with the others at the barbecue, which was

being run by Steph's father. As my turn came, he glanced up and bellowed, 'Ah, William. Now this looks like a man who won't say no to a sausage!'

I looked at the huge Cumberland that was being waved in front of my face and giggled.

'Go on,' my friend Tom said with a grin. 'You go get that sausage, William.'

'Thank you, Tom. And thank *you*, Clive,' I said. 'I will gladly take that sausage.'

Clive beamed. 'I knew it!' he said, triumphantly. 'See, Stephy!' he called over to his daughter. 'I knew William wouldn't say no to a sausage.'

Steph didn't hear him. She was too busy contemplating jumping off the roof with embarrassment.

I took the sausage and proceeded to laugh like a little girl with Tom for the next fifteen minutes, considering the different things we could say about the sausage and whether I should go back for seconds.

By way of a back story, I had just come out to my friends and family that summer that I was indeed a 'sausage lover'. It was a build-up of years of living a lie really and it was one of the most important moments of my life. That, winning *Pop Idol* and discovering that Michael Bolton and Kenny G had done an album . . . *together!*

I had known from the age of seven, I would say, that I was gay. When watching *Dallas* on television, I would get more excited by Bobby than Pam Ewing. I had little crushes on boys from school. I just knew – and with that knowledge, I carried what I felt was a dirty secret inside me for years and years. I played around with a boy once when I was about nine and I felt so ashamed of that throughout my time at prep school. It was always something that was seen as wrong – fundamentally wrong. I remember reading about Sodom and Gomorrah in Divinity lessons. In the story Lot and his family flee Sodom, a city where men are copulating with each other, on the eve of its destruction. It is depicted as a place of evil and sin, a godless society where everyone is going to hell. Lot's wife turns back when fleeing the city even though she has been warned not to by the angels who had come to destroy it, and she is turned into a pillar of salt. SALT! That's how evil this city was. The lesson was, clearly, that being gay was evil and wrong and you would go to hell. I carried this message with me for years. It burrowed deep into my psyche.

Moving on to public school I learned to hide any inkling of my being gay. The boys were bigger and scarier and school was not the place to walk around loud and proud.

Teenage boys are not known for their calm, comfortable understanding of their sexuality and hence an open-minded attitude to gay people! Being comfortable and open about my sexuality seemed like something I would never, ever be able to do. It is funny writing this now, as someone who is publicly out, quite literally, and as a pop star who was out from the beginning of his career. It is such a long way from the teenager who sat in his room at boarding school worrying about wearing the wrong shirt in case it was too gay.

Slowly, though, it dawned on me that it was something I had to deal with. It was making me extremely unhappy. I went to university and fell in love with a boy; it was unrequited but it was all the impetus I needed to get me to come out. The new friends I had made – who are still my friends today – accepted me and didn't care a bit. It was a revelation! I came out and was known as gay by everyone at university. I wasn't sexually active but I was out, and that was a huge thing for me.

My biggest fear after that was being seen as 'just another gay'. I'm afraid to say I looked down my nose at the LGBT Society and never dreamed of going to the one gay night down on the quay or the gay pub. No way! In truth, I was terrified of being labelled. I'd always hated that:

labelled as a twin, labelled as a public-school boy, labelled as gay. So instead I stayed away from it all. Not really the best move! I was sexually starved. While everyone else was bonking away merrily, I was probably the only out, gay young man in Exeter not getting any action. I was terrified of the act itself and I was terrified of rocking the boat, I guess. I was still 'Will who was gay but really could be straight' and that suited me just fine. Deep down, though, I was yearning for sexual contact and to really explore my sexuality.

I had a few tentative forays into the London gay scene. My first was a trip to G.A.Y. with someone from university who was bisexual. We met up in London and went out with his friend, who was very gay! Walking down Old Compton Street, I had never seen anything like it. There were gay men *everywhere*! I remember sitting in a café and spotting the most gorgeous boy I had ever seen . . . and he was gay; it was a revelation to me. There were men that could look so beautiful and be gay. Had they just dropped from heaven? Were they a gift from God? All I could do was stare.

From Soho, we went on to G.A.Y., which back then was in the now-demolished Astoria. I was appalled. All I could see were (probably married) men with younger men, who would no doubt slink back to their families when the night was over. Lewd, pervy older men buying drinks for pretty boys. This was enough for me. Was this what being gay was like? Not for me. Uh-uh. I would rather just carry on going to my usual haunts than be associated with people like that. Thinking back now, I just didn't see all the other gay men there who were simply having a good time. Such was my latent homophobia and fear in myself that all I could fixate on were the negatives and how people would perceive me. It depressed me. How was I going to fit into this world?

My next foray was just as unsuccessful. I went out with a friend's two sisters to the Freedom Bar in Soho. At first, this seemed a bit better than G.A.Y. People were vibier and the music was good. I saw a guy across the dance floor and the girls forced me to go up to him and offer to buy him a drink. I did it. It was terrifying. He also happened to be the only straight man in there. I couldn't believe it. I still bought him a drink because I was so embarrassed.

Neither of these trips into the London gay scene was a roaring success. The main aim, of course, was to get me a shag (!) but I didn't have the right mindset. And the London scene aside, I found the whole experience of being out terrifying. I didn't know how to act, what to be like.

I was just me, but should I be like someone else? Start wearing different clothes? Get gayer music taste? (Although I was always there for Kylie from the beginning. And Madonna was a given.)

It was the summer that I left university when I finally got some action. It came about through a summer job and it was brilliant. We didn't have full sex, but just to get some real physical contact after all those years was fantastic. Right, I remember thinking, if this is what it's going to be like from now on, then BRING IT ON!

I then started at ArtsEd and had a few dalliances there. Then things went a bit cold. I'm not going to delve into my whole sexual history, but it wasn't really until I went out with my second boyfriend that I really started to feel sexy and sexual as a person and that coincided with going out to more gay clubs. Discovering different gay clubs that I didn't even know existed. A whole different scene where people didn't just listen to Sugababes remixes and house music but great songs from The Cure to Blondie, David Bowie to The Stones. I am forever grateful for that relationship because although there was a lot of pain and home truths that I had to learn during that time, it performed a vital function . . . it got me out! I partied and it was fun. Christ knows I needed to do it. I had buried myself in work for years and it was time to get out there and enjoy myself.

That continued after the relationship. I carried on partying and had a great time. I met new people and I met other men and I'm not saying that was where I arrived at gay nirvana and suddenly everything was right with the world, because it wasn't. But I did start to get to grips with myself as a gay man and in the end this filtered into my work.

After I came out publicly, pretty much everyone then knew I was gay. It was a great moment and it was a great thing. I was happy to risk everything in order to remain true to myself and I am extremely proud of that decision. However, I remained aware that I was operating within a heterosexual mainstream and that overt gayness and pop success did not historically go together. So, effectively, I neutered myself. I would play down my gayness. When asked questions like 'Who would you like to kiss under the mistletoe?' I would never say a man. I would say... 'Beverly Knight'! In this, I was slightly guided by my management and the record company and not with bad intent. I myself wanted to downplay my sexuality because I knew if that became the overriding thing about me, then people would possibly not like it and I would become more threatening and less attractive as a pop star. And so, unwittingly, I became the pop star who was openly gay but who you could still take home to meet Mum – or even Gran – and he would never ever really allude to his gayness. He wouldn't sing about men. He wouldn't dress any differently and he was very polite!

In many ways I don't regret this, I didn't want my sexuality to overtake who I was. My point at the time – if there was one to be made – was that sexuality made no difference. I was still the same person, with the same voice. You could just be who you wanted to be. I think this was probably the right way to 'play the gay card'. And actually it wasn't made up or fabricated – I *was* fairly neutral sexually back then. I wasn't having full sex with anyone. I didn't have a boyfriend. And I certainly wasn't confident sexually or feel sexual. I was a bit like a doll. A very pretty doll!

Toeing the line at the beginning was actually quite fun. I would do a video wearing Speedos . . . but I would be learning to swim. So I played the pop star thing in some ways by getting my body out but then used comedy to hide it. It was enjoyable at that stage because I felt I could introduce an element of homo-erotica into my work without it affecting my mainstream appeal. This became more apparent when I did a video based on *Top Gun* for the song

'Switch It On'. There was always a well-known homo-
erotic sub-text in *Top Gun* and this was enhanced in the
video purely by the fact that I was a gay man pretending to
be the Tom Cruise character from the movie.

This is the amusing – but occasionally frustrating –
thing about sexuality. Sex is so pervasive in pop – it sits
behind the scenes, shaping everything. So just about
everything I did visually, particularly for my videos,
instantly acquired a sheen of homo-eroticism. I remember
for the video for 'All Time Love', the director, Wiz, was
keen for me to kiss a man. My concern was that it would
overshadow my music. Although, if I'm honest, looking
back, part of it was I just wasn't ready to take that risk. A
lot of people don't want to see a man kiss another man –
they just don't. This is the reality. And, to be fair to myself,
even if I were straight, I don't think I would have done a
video where I was kissing a girl, either. I just wasn't that
type of person.

The problem was that as time went on, I realised I
wanted to grow as a gay man. I wanted to explore aspects
of my sexuality and as this changed and I changed, I was
of course going to become more open and noticeably
sexual.

The crunch came a couple of years after 'All Time Love'

when I danced with a male mannequin for Wiz in a video for 'Let It Go'. It is one of my favourite videos, in fact. There was some quite strong opposition to me dancing with the top half of a male mannequin. Even while I was filming I knew there was going to be a reaction to it and I was intrigued to see how the record company were going to phrase this particular argument! They couldn't be seen to be homophobic, after all. I knew the wider social climate but I also knew I had reached a point where I felt it was the right thing to do creatively. I also felt more comfortable expressing my sexuality in a way I thought was interesting.

Anyway, the 'concerns' were raised, as expected, and the way it was phrased to me was that this one person who worked at Sony was anxious that my dancing with a mannequin might be picked up by the press as a reflection of the downturn in my sales and my success! I had to throw my phone away to stop myself ringing this person up!

The interesting thing is nowadays we don't even have these discussions. In the video for 'Jealousy' I am obviously in love with a man and I didn't question it even for a second. For 'Losing Myself', the first shot shows me and another man on my bed. I think the development has been a collective decision between me and the people I work with. As I have become more comfortable with who I am this has come out in my music and especially my videos – and I don't even think of the consequences.

It is the same with the clothes I wear and what I say. I enjoy wearing fashionable clothes and I feel far more confident in what I wear. I am no longer the boy who wore oversized jackets and wide-legged jeans with a hat to hide his face, sexually neutral and still having videos pitched at him where he was supposed to walk hand in hand down a beach with a girl, even though he was openly gay. (That was for 'Leave Right Now'. Can you *believe* that?)

Today I am at a stage where I am fully comfortable with being a gay man and a gay pop star. I have found the balance that is right for me and I am very proud of it. I am so proud that young boys and men can look at musicians, actors, politicians, business leaders, artists, people at all levels of all industries and see that there is nothing to fear. You can be whoever you want to be. That is the key. It is about finding what works for *you* that matters – not anybody else – and that is sure to involve some experimentation along the way. Being gay is only one part of my personality, but it took me years to realise that I should be proud of that part, rather than hide it away and be ashamed of it.

So, yes. I am Will Young. And yes, Clive, I will say yes to that sausage. Thank you very much!

LA down time

I find myself in Los Angeles. Sounds glamorous, doesn't it?
I am on a two-day writing trip then heading off to Sydney
for a week's holiday. In many ways, LA is the antithesis of
what I am about, yet I have fallen in love with it over the
years. To begin with it held the excitement of Hollywood,

the Kodak Theatre, Santa Monica Boulevard and Barneys. Later, it became a place where I would make friends, find my favourite shops and restaurants and lead quite a different life from the one I led in the UK. If anything, it was more glamorous. Nice restaurants, parties, fancy cars. LA has always felt more like a film than reality, in a way. I couldn't live there full time. But I do like to take a dip in the Hollywood pool occasionally.

The first time I came here was to perform on *American Idol* in the Kodak Theatre. Bizarrely, I also performed on *American Idol* the last time I was here. No one had heard of me the first time. I remember being introduced, and out of the whole theatre there were just a few small whoops, mainly from some friends who were in the audience, including Cathy Dennis, who had made a banner for me saying, 'GO WILL GO!' No one had heard of me the second time, either, and they largely played video clips over my performance. Cracking America is perhaps not part of my destiny.

Anyhow, back to Los Angeles. Because of its transitory nature, you can always meet interesting people. It is a place of broken dreams but also has that almost tangible possibility of success and fame in the air. On a more fickle note, the vintage shops are amazing and you can still smoke in some of the bars!

You can also get away with murder with an English accent. I once picked up some flowers from my manager from a shop in Hollywood. They were magnificent – the kind I imagine Jennifer Lopez receives daily. The people behind the counter asked me who I was to be sent such a beautiful bouquet. I turned on my heel and said, grandly, 'I'm royalty,' then swept out of the shop. In fact, I must have a royal complex because I told the cabbie who brought me here to the hotel that I am going to William and Kate's wedding. God, perhaps I am destined to be a conman. A royal one, though.

I have had some hysterical, bizarre moments in LA over the years. One of the finest was the meeting I had with a rather famous songwriter. I was working at the time with a wonderful man called Greg Kurstin, who in my opinion is one of the best and most exciting songwriters around. He started off with Beck, moved on to start his own band, The Bird and the Bee, and has penned songs for Kylie Minogue and Britney Spears, among others. Lily Allen used him to produce her entire last album. She spots the talent. He and Karen Poole, an English songwriter and a friend, had warned me of this person's unusual way of pitching her songs to artists. Apparently, she had different drawers that held different levels of pop song, and she would select a drawer depending on the 'calibre' of the artist who was visiting. The bigger the singer, the higher the drawer. I was fascinated by this idea and wondered which drawer I would be assigned. Probably the one in the loo. Anyhow, it didn't matter because, as I explained to Greg and Karen, I was not going for a formal pitching meeting but purely (or so I had been told by Jo McCormack, my lovely A&R lady) to have a coffee and chat. The idea of walking into a room and having songs pitched at me was horrific. I mean, I am happy to sing other people's songs – it hasn't harmed any of the great singers over the years, from Sinatra to Aretha – but choosing a song is like choosing an acting part. You have to feel an affinity with it, an ability to relate to the lyrics and express them in the right, honest way. No, I reiterated to Karen and Greg – this was not that kind of meeting. It was a 'get to know you' meeting. They smirked knowingly to themselves.

So, I arrived at this very grand office on Sunset and was shown into the room by a rather aloof assistant. I noticed a keyboard and, more ominously, a microphone set up next to a little swivel stool. This is odd, I thought. The songwriter came in, sat down on the swivel stool with her back to the microphone and immediately started telling me about a song she had just written. As the conversation continued about this song I managed to appear attentive on the outside, but on the inside I was thinking, Oh Christ, I hope she isn't going to sing. Please don't sing at me. I don't want you to sing at me. Oh no, she is going to sing at me. Sure enough, she swivelled around quick as anything, hitting the microphone perfectly, and began to belt out her song. Her voice was loud and the room was small and claustrophobic, so this was not a comfortable experience.

Me: (in my head) Oh God, oh God, oh God!

Her: 'Ooooohh baby . . .'

Me: (still in my head, but screaming now) Oh God, oh God, oh *God*! (Then, to the assistant, out loud this time) 'Do you sing backing vocals, then?'

She gazed at me, her expression ice cold. 'Occasionally.'

Oh God, oh God, oh my effing Christ.

I had to get out of there. This was living hell. I seethed. I am going to murder Jo McCormack, my no-longer lovely A&R lady. Murder her and then burn her house down.

After a verse and a chorus, I was asked, 'What do you think? Pretty great, huh? I mean, it's a hit, right?'

Strong words.

I replied, tactfully, that I found it hard to hear a song's

worth when it was being sung to me in close proximity (like five inches away).

'No problem,' replied the chanteuse. 'I have CDs with the songs on. Come through to my office.'

Shit. CDs?

Oh no – CDs from different drawers!

Different drawers dependent on the fame of the singer!

I know this. Karen and Greg told me about this. They were right. I was suddenly in the pitching session from hell.

And so it began. I was led into a huge office overlooking LA with lots of gold discs and leather furniture. Think Linda Barker meets HMV. They sat me in an armchair opposite the songwriter (in a larger chair) and the assistant put on the first song. With each song (the drawer was quite low down I noted; maybe number one was at the bottom), the assistant would put the CD in the machine, walk round to me and place a printout of the lyrics on my lap – without a word – then complete her silent circle by returning to the stereo and pressing play. The three of us would listen as far as the second chorus and then I would be asked for my opinion.

I was sweating profusely. With my various polite responses to each song, 'I don't think that one's for me', 'That one was great but perhaps not quite my thing', etc., the songwriter became more and more persistent. Finally, I stood up to the plate and confessed that I had been unaware that the meeting was going to be like this (like being sold some clothes on a rail – and not even good clothes – no soul, no heart, purely transactional) and told her it was making me uncomfortable. I apologised for any misunderstanding and said I thought it would be better if we just stopped and I left.

That did not get a great reaction.

The songwriter blew up. She said she'd had the best of the best in there and no one had *ever* said such a thing to her before. She also said she wrote the most soulful songs in the world. I desperately wanted to reply, 'Paul McCartney? Stevie Wonder?' but thought better of it. She was on a rant, and I could see it would not be wise to interrupt. When she finally finished shouting at me, she swept out of the room, the assistant following in her wake.

Now, this was awkward. Not only because I was left on my own in her huge office (and was sorely tempted to rifle through the other drawers) but because my rental car was in the building's car park and I didn't have a clue how to get to it. Twenty minutes later, after several visits to various floors, I found the car park, found my car and drove out. Not forgetting to call Jo and tell her she owed me the biggest pint she could ever imagine and that I wanted to murder her and burn her house down. She took it well.

I have had other dealings with big songwriters in America. My favourite was when I would arrive and they immediately handed me a CD of all their work but printed out like a normal album you would buy in a shop. What, no signed picture? I remember once crying to Faye, begging her not to make me do a writing session with these horrible people. I know now that she didn't want me to do it either, but at that stage we were both learning the ropes and playing the game to an extent. This happened a lot, particularly at the beginning of my career, until people realised that I didn't really like to work in this way.

I do completely understand that there is an air of commerce about pop music. I deal in mass-market music. It isn't edgy, I'm not going to change the way people perceive music. I know my limits and my capabilities. I am a pop singer who sings mainstream songs and likes to sell a lot of records. I don't see why that has to lead to the process becoming a soulless, purely money-driven experience. You can be mass market and still produce songs, videos and art-work that have depth and layers. For me, there still has to be an integrity to it. This has always been my belief and I realised a few years ago that I wouldn't be happy any other way – even if I sold more records – so I stuck by that deci-sion. I mean, if the work you are creating isn't fulfilling and doesn't make you happy, then what's the point?

Lecture over . . .

Now I'm going to pitch you some songs (swivel on stool and hit the microphone perfectly, with Faye singing back-ing vocals): this one is entitled 'I Want a Holiday Home in Barbados', the chorus kicks in at twenty-five seconds and doesn't stop repeating until . . . well, until the end.

'You've just got to bloody do it!'

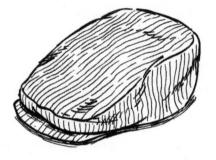

Lippo pointed at me, cigarette in one hand. 'There is no use complaining. You know you have to do it. So just bloody do it!'

We were in Aquarium, Steve Lipson's recording studio in Willesden. Hef (who mixes all of Steve's records) was sitting at his computer overlooking the recording booth at the end of the mixing desk. Steve was standing between his desk and the door. I was sitting at the other end of the room on a brown sofa. Sulking. Our familiar positions, both physically and emotionally. Steve was the protagonist and the deliverer of truth, Hef the defuser, and me the receiver/complainer/begrudging complier.

We were debating *World Idol*.

We have just made *Friday's Child*, my second record, in this studio. 'Leave Right Now', the first single, has come out and gone to number one. The album has sold a million copies in under four weeks.

To say all of this was unexpected is an understatement, because the knives had been out for me for at least a year. Such is the fickle nature of the business. One minute you're in, the next you're out, and you might not have done anything in between those two decisions. People get anxious. I had to re-record 'Leave Right Now' four times. The video, done by Kevin Godley of Godley and Creme fame, was a risk – very simple, one shot. But it all worked. Steve did a brilliant job with the production, and the video complemented the song perfectly.

This second album was do or die for me. It was the difference between having a career and melting away into obscurity. I had ridden the wave of publicity and coverage built up by twenty weeks of a TV talent show but now it was judgement day. I carried on mostly in blissful naivety.

In some ways I had no concept of failing. I don't think it was arrogance. It was two things – first, the legacy of the show and second, a refusal to even think about failure. My first single, 'Evergreen', charted at number one and sold 1.3 million copies in a week! The numbers were absurd. It was the fastest-selling single by a male debut artist and ended up being the best-selling debut single of the decade in the UK.

When this happened it didn't even register with me properly. I was so new to the game, I felt I had no hand in its creation. It was a cover of a song originally buried on a Westlife album. In fact, when I first heard it, I thought it was shit and said so (in a more polite way). We were still filming *Pop Idol*, and had reached the moment when the last three contenders were to be played the winning single. So it was me, Darius and Gareth in Olympic Studios in Barnes. It was a Sunday morning, Zoe Birkett had just been voted out the night before, and I was upset, fed up and tired. I couldn't even remember when we'd last had a day off. The final was coming ever closer, press exposure was building and – to be brutally honest – I had wanted Darius to go before Zoe.

The previous night, between rehearsals and the live show, Darius had come into the make-up room and asked me and Zoe if he should sit on a stool or on a chair turned backwards so his legs poked out either side. He was singing 'Whole Again' and one of the Atomic Kittens was in the audience. Zoe and I both suggested at the same time that he should use the chair. He thanked us – although we could see the suspicion in his eyes – and left. Zoe turned to me and said, 'Well, I need all the help I can get!' She was joking, of course – we knew Darius would do what Darius wanted to do, whatever answer we gave. But what was interesting was that this was the only time in all of those weeks of live shows that I ever heard anyone alluding to who might be voted off that week. We weren't often surprised, but none of us ever spoke about it and, genuinely, no one ever tried to harm or damage someone else's chances. We really were there for each other. Even Darius, who was a good game player, was never malicious and kind of operated in his own world. The rest of us just got on with it, which made for a great atmosphere.

Anyway, Darius went for the stool option instead and Zoe went home. The next day I found myself in Olympic Studios, waiting to listen to and record the two songs that would make up the double A-side winner's single. One was called 'Anything Is Possible', written by Cathy Dennis, and the other was by some Swedish people. Cathy's was Simon Fuller's choice; the Swedish/Westlife one was Cowell's. Gareth Gates was a huge Westlife fan and was getting to sing . . . a Westlife song. I was a Cathy Dennis fan of old but unfortunately 'Anything Is Possible' did not match up to her heritage of songwriting in my opinion. Darius could sing neither of the songs because they were in the wrong keys for his voice and they weren't going to change them – which was absurd! I mean, poor Darius! The keys to the songs were perfect for Gareth's voice, which was the highest of the three of us.

For the filming we were required to walk into the studio for 'Evergreen' (I don't think we filmed in Cathy's studio downstairs). Simon was standing there along with the Swedish songwriters (who were very nice), awaiting our reactions once we'd been played the song. Cameras roll and we're off. I'm tired and upset and standing in a room with the judge I least like. The song finishes. The camera turns to Simon, then me. Simon asks, 'What do you think, Will?'

I respond, 'I'd rather shit in a bucket.' (Of course, I *don't* say this. But I am thinking it. 'It isn't really my kind of song' is what I actually say.)

There is an awkward pause and the director calls 'cut'.

These two songs were so out of line with what Darius and I had been singing on the show. 'Evergreen', in particular, really did seem to have been hand-picked for Gareth, given its Westlife heritage. And this was going to be the song that the victor sang immediately after winning!

It was at this point that I began to give up hope of winning and became a little disillusioned with the process, to be honest. The songs felt more like a final hurdle to jump over than something to be enjoyed. In fact, the whole final became a bit like that. The show had been going on a long, long time by now. The dream of getting a record contract felt attainable, so in a way I had done what I set out to do. These songs – that felt so far away from what I was listening to or singing on the show – became like processes that I had to get through, to get to what I really wanted to do.

Incidentally, in time 'Evergreen' has of course become more about a moment than the tune itself and to be fair to Simon Cowell he said that to me and he was right. Now when I do sing it, it's often a highlight of the show because it takes people right back to that final again. It also makes me feel young and bountiful . . . like an evergreen tree.

After 'Evergreen' charted I went on the *Pop Idol* tour,

which started off as a seven-date arena tour and ended up being thirty-six dates. My very first gig was at Wembley Stadium. How amazing!

On the tour there was an instruction that we all had to stay in hotels outside the cities. That directive came right from the top – Simon Fuller. Here was a sign of how he had managed S Club Seven and the Spice Girls – with a calm but highly effective iron rod. It was funny, even at the beginning we were always aware of Simon's presence and reach, but we never saw him. Often I would hear, 'We are doing this because of Simon,' and I would think, Who *is* this man? We would ask, why can we only stay in hotels in the countryside? Who made up this rule? Answer: Simon Fuller. Oh, right. And that was that – we all went along with it. He effused this air of authority, even though we hardly ever met him.

Whenever we did he was always surrounded by very efficient, glamorous women who all worked for 19 Management. They were always extremely professional, although I had a run-in early on with one of them, who asked me to remove my flat cap during the final week of *Pop Idol*. The message came from headquarters via Faye (who had started working with me that week): the flat cap had to go. I was twenty-two, had been to university, had my own sense of style (maybe not the best style, but it was mine!) and suddenly other grown-ups were telling me how to dress. I stood my ground and that pretty much set the benchmark for the next ten years!

Right from the start, I was very mindful of the pop world and worried that people might try to turn me into something I wasn't. Over the years my style and my appreciation of fashion have changed dramatically, but at the time I was just being true to who I wanted to be then and actually this also worked in my favour on the show. It would not have been truthful to start dressing as someone completely different – and it would have been a huge mistake, too. I remember a message coming through from the record company a year later that simply asked, 'Is Will actually wearing any of the clothes that are being bought for him?' The idea was to give me a budget for work clothes and then another one to build up a wardrobe of personal clothes that were better than the ones I owned! They must have been going mad at the record company. I would often end up in the 'How Not to Dress' category. I once appeared in the same magazine for best-dressed and worst-dressed – in the same outfit!

Even if I thought I was dressing like an effortlessly cool person but looked like someone who had crashed into a second-hand clothes shop, it didn't matter. The most important thing was the music.

Flat cap arguments aside, it was these directives from Simon Fuller, channelled through these glamorous strong women, that led me to firmly believe that he was Charlie from *Charlie's Angels*. I even imagined the little seventies speakerphone sitting on his desk in Battersea. All we see is a perfectly manicured hand pressing a button and then . . .

'Tell them they can only stay in countryside hotels.'

And even though we don't see his face, we know that Charlie/Simon is actually Blake Carrington from *Dynasty*.

So we stayed in these countryside hotels and all went slowly mad. I know Simon was just trying to protect us from our sudden exposure to the spotlight. He didn't want us falling out of every nightclub throughout the UK, getting photographed and perhaps not being in the safest of environments. It was a crazy situation. The reaction from certain members of the public could at times border on the manic. I remember four of us wanted to go for a shop around Leeds. There was a great indoor market that I wanted to visit and then we went to get some lunch from Marks and Spencer. As more and more people spotted us, crowds started to form and in the end people were backed up outside the window of M&S. The security guards we

had brought with us had to call the tour bus and we had to make our escape through the screaming crowds into the waiting bus. This would happen at motorway service stations, too. Gareth and I once had to escape out of the back of the men's loos. As I clambered out of the window at Sedgemoor Service Station, I thought, Not *quite* what I envisioned when I entered *Pop Idol*.

So I could understand the concern for our safety, but we were all young, we had come into some money, some fame and we wanted to GO OUT! I would sometimes play a game in the day time to try to escape the security guards, but they would always be waiting for me. I remember once even putting on a chambermaid's housecoat and attempting to sidle past security and out of the hotel but to no avail. So, instead, I would end up having a coffee on my own while one of the guys would sit at the table next to me. It was the most awkward situation and because I often wanted to get out and see a town or have some time to myself, this would happen regularly!

It became a battle. Once, in Glasgow, we had a night off and we were allowed to go out... but only to a pre-approved venue. I started the evening by chatting up a (straight) member of a boy band – but it got me warmed up. He was a friend of Jessica Garlick's, and after two drinks I had started stroking him. When he finally managed to evade me I was hitting full steam and moved to the dance floor with Zoe. But after a few minutes I could smell something funny.

I shouted to Zoe, 'What's that smell?'

'Dunno, babe,' she replied.

We carried on dancing until Zoe started screaming that my hair was on fire. I had lit a cigarette, placed it behind my ear and promptly set my hair alight. This was the cue for security to swoop in. We were whisked out and I spent the whole journey back to one of our countryside retreats telling Malcolm the security guard that all I wanted was a shag. When we arrived I rang Jessica's room and – in between sobbing that no one understood what a *prison* my life had become – asked if I could have that boy band guy's number as it would make me feel much better. She complied. I texted to ask him for a shag. He said no. I passed out.

On reflection, perhaps this was why Simon didn't want us to go out!

And so the tour went on in a mêlée of failed escapes and a few carefully controlled nights out, often ending in a hastily aborted disco when one of us got too cheerful.

Then it was on to my second single, 'Light My Fire'. This sold around half a million in the end and went to number one. Then there was a duet with Gareth that also went to number one and sold around two hundred thousand copies. Followed by another arena tour that sold out. And then my fourth single, which went to number two.

I am throwing these stats at you to show why I became so used to a ridiculous amount of success. Number ones just seemed like a given. In fact, I remember getting in a strop when the head of Sony, Ged Doherty, laughed at me predicting a million sales for 'Light My Fire'! I didn't know any different. I was super, super naive and didn't know or realise the importance of getting this first song for the second album right. If it bombed, I might never get a second chance.

Part of the deal of winning *Pop Idol* was that I signed to
Simon Cowell's label, BMG. I don't suppose that was ever
going to work out, for obvious reasons. But I must admit I
found it a bit surprising when the head of my own record
label – who was making a lot of money out of me –
snubbed me in public. On *Newsround*, no less! Isn't that
brilliant? To be snubbed by Simon Cowell on *Newsround*?
If John Craven had still been hosting it, I think I would have
died happy. (Although *Countryfile* would run it a close
second. Imagine if I'd been slagged off by Simon Cowell on
Countryfile! In fact, that would be even better!)

Anyway, after Simon's star appearance on *Newsround*, the
bosses of BMG rang to apologise. I honestly had no axe to
grind with Simon, but I did find his animosity towards me
quite stressful. All I wanted was to build a long-term career,
develop my voice and keep my head straight in the midst
of becoming – overnight – one of the most recognisable
young men in the UK. Although I do remember warning
him that if he ever tried to sabotage my career he would
regret it! (Quite what I thought I was going to do I'm not
sure but I applaud the intention. Maybe I planned to retal-
iate through some other meteorite of a kids' show, like *Blue
Peter* or the *Teletubbies*.)

In the end, when things didn't really improve, Simon

Fuller moved me within BMG to RCA. With a new label as a home and battles with the Cowell over, it was time for a new album and the next person to change my life around was by no means average . . . Steve Lipson.

'If I don't do this, you won't have a career'

We met at the Anglesey Arms in Chelsea. It was near where I was living at the time while my house in Holland Park was being done up. Quite a leap from being a student in Exeter. I couldn't believe it. In the space of a year and a half I had left university and was renovating a house in Holland Park and I was about to have lunch with Steve Lipson, the guy who had produced Annie Lennox's *Diva* album and had worked with Whitney Houston, Frankie Goes to Hollywood, the Art of Noise, Grace Jones . . . the list went on and on. Quite a leap from attempting and failing the splits in Turnham Green.

I was hung over. The previous night I had gone to a gay night at Fabric. The evening started with me playing kiss chase with buses and ended at 6 a.m. with me and some friends playing our own version of jousting that involved pushing each other in wheelie bins down the Fulham Road.

I was also mega stressed with the album. I had written quite a few songs in Ireland, again with songwriters Bif and Julian. I had gone down the Norah Jones route. I thought the songs were okay.

I met Lippo in the back. He is a tall, slim-framed man with piercing, intelligent eyes that take in everything.

'You look rough,' he said. 'Hi, I'm Steve.'

'Thanks. Hi, I'm Will.'

'We have actually met before. I did the *Pop Idol* big band album, remember?'

'Yes.'

'Great. Right, I'll get to it. I want to do your album because I think you are really good . . . and because if I don't do your album no one is going to look after you and you won't have a career.'

I was quite taken aback by the drama of this delivery. I didn't think the situation was *that* bad. Maybe it was? Shit. What I did know was Steve Lipson believed in me enough to come and meet me and tell me so, and I needed that. I needed a producer who believed in me, saw what I could do as a recording artist *and* called a spade a spade. Steve most definitely called a spade a spade.

After that initial meeting I went to his studio in Willesden and I met Hef, who as I mentioned mixed all of Lippo's work. They worked as a team. In time I would hear wild tales of Bobby Brown and Whitney Houston, fantastic stories of working with Annie Lennox in America . . . but here I was first day in Aquarium and Lippo wanted to hear what I had written so far.

I played ten songs. He didn't like any of them.

I remember him saying, 'What *is* this? I mean what *are* they?'

'I dunno . . . They are songs. I like them.'

'Well, I don't. And I tell you what, if you think these are going to give you a career then you are wrong. Oh, Christ. Can I be honest with you?'

'You mean you're not being honest with me now?'

'We have to start from scratch. These songs aren't good enough. We've got a lot of work to do. *You've* got to start writing more and that's that. Oh, and we need a hit single.'

I liked him. I still do. In fact, he has become a father figure to me. He is direct, he is honest and he is very smart. He gets it. He gets what the business is about and he gets good music. He also gets excited and that excites me. If someone I trust gets excited then so do I, even if I don't understand what they are getting excited about, because it means they are seeing something and that means we are on the right track. Often I have worked with people and I haven't seen what it is they are seeing in a song or in my delivery or in a video idea or photoshoot, but if I trust the person then I know something is working out! Steve got excited, he got tough and honest, but he was also seeing something that could be achieved and I felt that I had found someone who I should hang on to. Someone who was going to help me out.

This leads me to my other point about where my head was at with this album. Along with not being used to any kind of 'bad results' thanks to the show, I also just didn't foresee the album not working. I guess I had this core belief/naive thought that it would all be fine. I have to say this has never left me. I try not to think too much about what would happen if it all goes wrong, if no one likes the songs and the label drops me. I just get on with it and try to be as truthful to myself as I can be and then, hopefully, it will work. It sounds facile in some respects, but I think the alternative is to become so paralysed with fear that I wouldn't ever do anything again. If I thought about all the what-ifs and scenarios where things could go wrong, I don't think I'd ever finish an album.

The aim with the second album was really to become

established and show that I was going to stick around. It was 'Leave Right Now' that gave me that chance and ironically, I didn't even want to record it originally. It was written by Eg White, with whom I was writing some of the album anyhow and he was so patient about my opinion of it – I felt it was too downbeat and I wanted to do something more high energy.

I remember Lippo saying to me, '*This* is the song you have to do, and you are making a big mistake if you don't.' Simon Fuller also saw the song's potential, as did Jo McCormack and her husband Mike, who was publishing Eg at the time . . . but I didn't. I was too fixated on a change of sound, rather than putting out a great song. In my head I felt dull and uncool. I sang nothing but ballads. I wasn't really doing anything of any artistic merit. And now I was going to put out a slow boring song called 'Leave Right Now'? As one BMG executive said (he doesn't know I know this!), 'I can see the headlines: "Will *should* leave right now . . . for good."' So I wasn't the only one who was nervous and untrusting of this song.

Thankfully enough people I trusted had huge belief in the song and I listened to them. Now I look back, I realise that my approach in many ways was all wrong. Even as I write I can see how crucial Steve's role was in doing exactly as he promised – 'giving me a career in pop'. I am forever grateful to him because what happened with 'Leave Right Now' did give me a career in pop and a lot more besides.

'You've got *Parky*,' said Faye.

'No?'

'Yes! You have got *Parky*!'

From *Pop Idol* to *Parky* was quite a thing. *Parkinson* was still the crème de la crème of chat shows. Everyone had been on – from Muhammad Ali to Joan Crawford to Kenneth Williams... *everyone*. It was a thing of TV legend. I would perform 'Leave Right Now' and there would be no interview, but that suited me fine, because the prospect was slightly terrifying. Actually looking back now, I was right to be terrified! If I'd known how much rode on this performance, I don't think I would have been able to open my mouth, never mind sing.

A few weeks before the show I had put together a biography 'catch-up' to go with the album with top music journalist Neil McCormick. Whenever an artist releases a new record they always put out a new biography – a sort of refresher of what has been going on, a general interview on the ideas behind the record and anything else of interest. This is then condensed into a blurb and sent out in the press pack. I got on really well with Neil and was very candid with him. He wrote the blurb and that – I thought – was that.

But then, on the day *Parkinson* was due to be recorded, Neil wrote a glowing half-page review of the album in the *Telegraph*, saying that if he had a hat, he would eat it. It really couldn't have been any better. Neil was one of the most respected music journalists in the country . . . and he had torn *Pop Idol* to pieces in the past. So this vote of approval was staggering. The headline for the piece was 'All Hail the New President of Pop'!

Michael Parkinson read the review and decided that I should be interviewed as well as sing! Suddenly things were rolling. I sang (very nervously) and found myself being interviewed sitting alongside Judi Dench and Peter Kay. I told Parky that I would like to do some acting one day and before a year had passed I was in a film with Judi Dench herself! (This was thanks to *Parkinson* as well, because the film's musical director, George Fenton, saw the show.)

After my appearance on *Parky* other people started writing retractions of things they had said about me and *Pop Idol*. I now realise that Lippo and I had done exactly what we had set out to achieve – namely to create an album of real pop class that truly surprised everyone. It was such a change of gear from the first album and I am ever-thankful for the way things played out. Because if it hadn't been for that chain of events – from Steve saying he wanted to help me to him insisting I should record 'Leave Right Now' to Neil McCormick writing that review to Parky deciding to interview me – I am sure I would not have a career today. We all need a few things to go our way sometimes, we all need a few gates to open, and that certainly happened with *Friday's Child*.

From there it was ever upwards. I went from a theatre tour to an arena tour to landing that part in the film *Mrs Henderson Presents*. I released three singles, all with brilliant and very different videos. It was an amazing success story. But the sad thing is that I didn't have the time – or the ability – to enjoy it. I worked so hard and wanted this success so much, but I didn't appreciate at the time how great it was. And I guess I didn't really think I deserved it.

When I came to do my next album, this lack of self-belief and confidence was to rise to the fore and create problems.

Keep On

After a short break I started work on my 'difficult' third album with Steve. And it was difficult. I was so hyper-aware of trying to do something different. I didn't want to come back with another ballad, for instance. For some reason I was *obsessed* with the fact that I was known only for singing ballads, even though my two most recent hits – after 'Leave Right Now' – had actually been mid-tempo. I was also transfixed by all the negative things that might be said about me. I wanted to be cool. I wanted to be in Q magazine and hang out with hipsters and write life-changing music. It made the whole album a struggle.

One good thing that came out of all this was that I did explore things far more as a songwriter. I wrote loads of different styles of songs, which was an important process for me. It was something I had to go through – and you can't fast-forward experience, you just have to live through it. I worked with loads of great people – from Nitin Sawhney to Dan Carey to Andy Cato, all three of them amazing musicians and producers – and I learned a lot.

I was adamant that the first single shouldn't be slow, so I really fought to go with 'Switch It On'. The album –

Keep On – got to number two and the single reached number five, but I didn't feel content. I remember performing on *Parky* again and I was like a different person. I had become arrogant and so hyper-sensitive to criticism that I had toughened up – partly to protect myself. I tried to be cool and aloof rather than the 'lovable nice Will Young' that everyone knew . . . and I despised. 'Nice' was bad. The people who *really* got the coverage and the respect were cool offhand celebrities, not a guy who treats people well and talks posh. In short, I became an arsehole – and very difficult to work for.

I was also hating work. I felt creatively stuck and I lacked confidence as a live performer. It was all falling apart, really. On top of this I had started going out with someone and that was throwing up a whole load of issues I had about intimacy, who I was as a gay man, and how I truly acted in my life. Friends will put up with all this stuff, as will family, and if you are your own boss you don't necessarily have to face things at work, either (although Faye would be quite happy in the end to tell me how I was acting!). But with a relationship you can't ignore your problems. If I was a workaholic then it became clear. If I was desperately insecure then it became clear. If I was sometimes offhand with people and lacking in confidence it became clear. And it *did* all become clear.

This is when I first started therapy. I was lucky enough to be in a job that was also my passion, but I was beginning to hate it and feel that I was shit at it. From the outside, I appeared so successful, but I had huge problems with who I was as a person, which had knock-on effects in every area of my life. I ran the risk of fucking up everything – ending up with no career, not being comfortable with who I was and becoming rather sad and bitter in the process. Things had to change.

And they did.

Let It Go was the title of my fourth album and also the mantra I learned along the way.

I finished *Keep On* with my second arena tour. I had made a rather unfortunate decision to maximise the creative output for the tour and minimise my profit! In essence, I made no money *at all*! Ten out of ten for artistic integrity, nought out of ten for business nous.

After the tour I went to Manchester to play the lead in *The Vortex* by Noël Coward. I was very unhappy during this period. I broke up with my boyfriend and was drinking and smoking too much. The character I was playing, Nicky Lancaster, is pretty much despised by everyone else in the play. He's also a musician and a precocious upstart.

Probably not a million miles away from real life at that stage. Diana Hardcastle, the actress who played my mother in the play, was a lifeline for me, though. She was incredibly kind and supportive over my personal problems. I was a nightmare; so desperately unhappy.

After that I decided to run around the world, avoiding my heartache and sadness. I had some good times but the sadness was still there, waiting for me, when I returned. I got back together with my boyfriend, then broke up with him again. And then I started the new album. It was cathartic and it was healing. My approach to work had completely changed and the whole process was far more relaxing. I had learned to shield myself more at work. When people offered their opinions, as they often did, this protective layer stopped any criticism from sending me mad. I also realised that treating people well and being kind and decent was no bad thing, and didn't mean that I couldn't be firm and assertive when needed. And with my job hanging in the balance, it finally hit home that it was the thing I loved doing the most – and I would be damned if I was going to mess it up.

I opened at Glastonbury and played festivals throughout the summer. The single 'Changes' did well and *Let It Go* went to number two. I was safe. I wasn't out of the woods . . . but I was safe. I started playing with a different band and began to feel more confident on stage. I started having fun, too! Interestingly, the reviews for my live dates got better as well.

I still had a way to go. I was too caught up with trying to impress others outside work. But within work I was finding my feet. I was becoming more confident, and when that little voice inside my head told me I was crap at my job, I reminded myself that actually I was pretty damn good at it! When the voice said, 'James Morrison is selling more than you, you are rubbish,' I would just ignore it. It was easier that way. When the voice said, 'God, you look old' – I was only twenty-nine! – 'and you should be selling more records and filling bigger venues than Robbie Williams,' I knew now that this got me nowhere and – again – ignored it. Slowly, I found some stability at work and it makes me smile just thinking about the difference that made. People would comment on how relaxed the Will Young 'team' was, and how happy we all looked. Well, of course! That's because they weren't worrying every five seconds about how I was going to react. I might not have found real happiness just yet, but I was starting to appreciate the true meaning of being a professional. No one else took their personal problems into work, so why should I? And what is more, work actually gave me the perfect space to express my frustrations and fears, so why would I jeopardise that?

After *Let it Go* came the *Greatest Hits* album. It wasn't necessarily something that I wanted to do at that stage but the record company were keen. My sales had dipped considerably in comparison with *Keep On* and I guess they weren't happy. At one stage it looked like I might be leaving them. Funnily enough, I wasn't stressed by this. I just thought, Well, if it happens, then I guess I'll go somewhere else. Or not! Either way, I felt like I could get some sort of work and I had a house and some money in the bank.

In the end, I agreed to go ahead and as it turned out it was great fun. It also did really well for a hits album and bought me some time with Sony. My crazy years – in a work sense, at least – were left behind. I toured again. And I got a part in *Bedlam*, a TV drama. It was hard work … and I loved every minute of it. Three months' filming in Manchester with a lovely group of people.

It was in Manchester that I put the finishing touches to *Echoes*, my new album. I'd wanted to do an electro-pop album for years, and now at last I got my chance. I was a big fan of Steve Mason's album *Boys Outside*, produced by

Richard X. It was beautifully done. I wrote to Richard and asked if he would produce mine and he said yes!

With *Echoes*, I felt like I really was completely in the right place. Everything seemed to happen so easily, from Richard coming on board, writing with Jim and Mima of Kish Mauve, the photoshoot in New York with the amazing Guy Aroche to the video to the TV special where I got to work with producer Michael Gracey and choreographer Ashley Wallen again. It was a natural, fun process and it felt like exactly where I should be.

And this is work to the present day. From *Pop Idol* to *Cabaret* with a lot in between. I can't imagine what the next ten years of work will be like – and that's a good thing! I'm proud of myself for getting on top of the insanity that is being a pop star – and everything that goes with it. It was not easy . . . and yet, in another way, it was actually the easiest decision to make because if it wasn't for my career, I'm not even sure I would still be around. If it wasn't for the music, I would have no connection to what really matters – being in the moment and acting naturally. That is what singing does for me. It allows me to be spiritually connected. To make a million choices a minute without really thinking about it. Music is quite simply my saviour, and the longer I do this, the more I appreciate and respect it.

As Lippo said all those years ago: 'You've just got to bloody do it!'

Oh . . . and I did do *World Idol*. I came seventh.

'Could you sign my arm, please? I've just got out of prison'

'She's coming towards you.'

'I know.'

'Just look to your right and you'll see her.'

'I don't want to, Faye.'

'Go on, do it. Go ON! You're in for a treat.'

'I'm scared.'

'You should be.'

Faye is giggling. A lot. We are standing just off the Edgware Road on a sunny afternoon in May. Our task for the afternoon is prowling every charity and seconds shop in the area stretching from Marylebone High Street to Kilburn High Road. We are on the hunt for 250 T-shirts and 250 pairs of trousers to create a backdrop for some summer shows I am doing. These are known as 'forest shows' and interviewers keep asking me about 'singing in forests'. And every time I'm asked, I find I can't take the upcoming tour seriously because it makes me sound like a cross between Robin Hood and someone cottaging. The posters could read:

COME AND SEE WILL IN A WOODLAND!

WILL YOUNG, COMING TO A WOOD NEAR YOU . . . SOON.

NO, SERIOUSLY. HAVE YOU SEEN THIS MAN? HE MIGHT BE SINGING IN YOUR LOCAL WOODS . . . IN TIGHTS.

STAY WELL CLEAR.

Faye and I have bought out most of West London's shops (except the Sue Ryder on Marylebone High Street, which we have discovered is packed with designer cast-offs and is hence very expensive) and have taken a moment to rest on a side road opposite Edgware Road tube station. It is from here that my fan emerges.

I hear her before I see her. There is a soft thump, followed by the sound of scraping metal and then little gasps accompanying the scrapes. This cycle continues a few times before I am forced to look. A middle-aged woman – in her late forties, perhaps – is heading slowly but determinedly towards me. She is in a wheelchair. So far, so normal. The soft thumps, however, are caused by her slippered feet rising then hitting the floor in front of her, then rolling on her heels, which act as leverage to drag her and the wheelchair forward. It is one of the strangest sights I have seen in quite a while. A lady who has obviously 'lived', sitting in a wheelchair but with full use of her legs, dragging herself towards me. The look on her face is one of pure focus and delight. Her tongue hangs out to one side in concentration.

Faye and I are rooted to the spot.

'She's a-coming for you.'

'I can see that, Faye, thank you.'

The whole thing takes about ten minutes but I don't feel

that I can spoil it by walking over to her – and I certainly can't leave.

Thump, scrape, heavy pant. Thump, scrape, heavy pant.

Faye tilts her head, impressed. 'She's pretty close now.'

Thump, scrape, pant. Thump, scrape, pant.

Finally the lady arrives in front of us. 'I knew it was you! I knew it! I told you it was him, Keith,' she shouts back to her friend, sitting in a doorway. 'Well, how lovely to see you. Now, could you sign my arm, please? I've just got out of prison.'

The thing is, fans are fans. All fans – so long as they are polite – are brilliant and I don't write this to remain PC or say the right thing. They are. They buy my records, they allow me to do what I love. How can I be anything other than grateful? Now, of course, this doesn't mean that every time I see a fan I should get down on my knees, sob and thank them from the bottom of my heart for allowing me to sing for a living and giving me the leeway to buy a rug from the Rug Company. No. There is, of course, a line.

There are all sorts of fans as well. There are the quiet ones. The ones who might just send a note to my table if I am eating. Or buy me a drink. I remember once, I wasn't having the best of days. I'd been wandering along the King's Road towards the Bluebird Café, *Friday's Child* had just come out and was doing great . . . and then some boys called me a fag – shouted it across the street. They could easily have been boys I'd played rugby against a few years before. Suddenly I wasn't feeling my best.

I ordered a coffee and along with my coffee arrived a rose with a note attached saying: '"You got wings but you can't fly" is a beautiful lyric.'

I looked around for the person who had sent the flower and the card but couldn't see anyone. I still have this note – it lived on my mantelpiece in my old house for six years. That person turned my day around and moments like that can give me months of energy to carry on. Whoever it was had really liked something that I had written, had listened so intently to the song that they had picked out that line, and had taken the time and thought to tell me how much they appreciated it. You just can't ask for anything more than that. That is what everyone wants in life. All I need is two or three moments like that a year and I feel protected against all the unpleasant things I might come across.

Other notes are accidentally brilliant. One of my favourite letters came from a nine-year-old girl, who wrote to me just after I came out. It read: 'Dear Will, I like your music. Why have you said that you are gay? I am worried you will never get a girlfriend now.'

But then there are other fans. Less subtle fans. These people are a little crazy. Letters are written. Presents are sent. Some think they are having a full-on relationship with me.

There was a girl who for the year or so immediately after *Pop Idol* would write to me as if we were having a relationship. I will call her Pat Brown. She would write, usually from Scotland, about our impending marriage, where we should live and indeed what my family thought about this whole affair. Faye would read the letters and keep them (just in case!), so she was well aware of the situation.

One night I appeared on a show and after pre-recording the performance (I think it might have been 'Light My Fire') I was leaving the studios when a girl approached. Faye was busying herself a couple of yards away with someone from the production company so I'd been left on my own.

'Hi Will.'

'Hello,' I replied, looking at the girl and thinking, I'm sure I recognise her.

'Hi Will.'

'Er . . . hello,' I repeated. Perhaps she didn't hear me the first time? I glanced over my shoulder towards Faye.

'HI WILL,' said the girl again. This time more firmly. *Uh oh.*

'Hello?' I replied, followed by a quick little chirp towards Faye. 'Fayeee,' I called lightly, essentially saying, in that one word, 'Faye, I think this girl might be mad. Faye, please help me. Faye, is this girl packing a piece? Faye, where is the car? Faye, HELP!'

The girl was staring intently at me. I decided I should keep her talking. Perhaps it would distract her from pulling the machete that I was sure she was hiding under her smock.

'So . . . how are y—'

'I'm sure you are wondering who I am,' she interrupted. 'I'm a big fan, Will. BIG fan. I've always wanted to meet you and today I just thought to myself, Today is the day I am going to meet Will. So I came down here. I haven't told my parents. I just came down here and now I am just so excited to meet you. Like I said, I am your BIGGEST FAN.'

As she said all this, the speed of her delivery became more and more rapid. On top of that, her body was beginning to shake. It was like that chemistry lesson when the teacher puts the ping-pong balls on the overhead projector to show how atoms change when heated up. A machine vibrates them and the faster it goes the more the ping-pong balls/atoms shake around. This girl's atoms were definitely vibrating. But, as well as shaking and talking louder and faster, she was slowly lifting something out of the bag that was hanging across her front.

'You know,' she continued, even faster, 'ever since I saw you on *Pop Idol* I knew, I JUST KNEW, that you were going to win. I've got all your letters and I think Gareth Gates is just shit. SHIT! SHIT! You are the one and only pop idol and I will always support you – always.' Pause. Deep breath. 'I like your skin.'

My body has frozen with fear. I am thinking, Move your bloody legs, William – move them. But for some reason they remain where they are. I call over to Faye again – 'Fayeeeeee, oh Fayeeee – *do* come over here, would you?' Faye is trying her best to extricate herself from the production assistant, who is getting her to sign even more forms.

Then everything happens in slow motion.

'I came to get this,' the girl says. She is clutching the object she pulled out of her bag in both hands now, and raising it to her chest. She is visibly shaking all over and the tremor is detectable in her voice.

I'm too distracted to see what she's holding but suddenly something dawns on me. Could it be? Oh my God, it might be . . .

'What is your name?' I ask.

Faye has half-turned towards me and is signing contracts almost behind her back now. Her ears are straining for the reply. I can see she has had the same thought.

'My name?' the girl replies, hands still rising so the object is by her chin.

'Yes, your name.'

I wait. My legs have turned to jelly.

'My name . . . is Pat Brown.'

Pat Brown. PAT BROWN!! FUUUUUCCCCKKKK! It's PAT SHITTING BROWN!

I gasp. I hear Faye gasp too and see her drop all her paperwork as she rushes over. Everything has gone film-like. Suddenly there is a loud sharp click and a furious winding sound. I look at Pat and the object she is holding. It is an old-fashioned instant wind-on camera.

Oh God.

'Hello Will.' *Click.* 'Smile for the camera. Smile for Pat, Will.'

All decorum has gone. Faye begins to bundle me into the waiting Mercedes that has just that second turned up. Pat is still taking photos, *very close* photos of my face, at a furious speed, clicking and frantically whirring away as I am being ushered into the car. Click, wind, click, wind, click, wind. I leap into the car and the door slams shut, but

I can still hear Pat's instant camera. The window isn't tinted so Pat rests the camera lens against it and takes photo after photo. But she's holding the camera at tummy level and I realise she isn't looking through the viewfinder. She is just staring at me while clicking and winding her camera.

I must say, even writing this I am experiencing a light perspiration on my top lip. The image of Pat Brown leaning against the back window, pressing her instant camera against the glass, constantly taking photos while gazing intently at me, has stayed with me to this day. That and the time I glimpsed Judy Finnigan's laddered tights (back right thigh) when I was on *This Morning*.

I feel a close connection with my fans, but it's taken me a while to get to grips with it all. I went from being completely unknown to playing in front of huge audiences . . . and I had no idea how to communicate with any of them! I mean, how *do* you talk to thousands upon thousands of people without sounding like an arse? I cannot bear it when I hear American pop stars (who often seem to have taken a degree in insincerity) standing on a stage, trolling out the sentence: 'You know . . . if it wasn't for you guys I wouldn't be here. I just think the fans in (glance down at card) . . . the fans in Nottingham (pronounced Not-ting-*ham*) are the best in the world! I love you. I love you like I love my Prozac.'

Who hears that and doesn't want to be sick all over themselves? I don't want to hear someone telling me that if it wasn't for me, they wouldn't be there. No, I want them to get on stage, sing the songs, not talk about anything political, and then get off again. Then my little bubble of perfection for them lives on.

The thing is, due to my route into music, it really *can* be said quite literally that if it wasn't for my fans, I would not have a career. Because it was thanks to the people who voted for me that I had a chance to be a pop star. No record company execs or A&R people decided my fate. It was the British public from the beginning. There was an ownership that was more apparent.

There have been times when I have been completely freaked out by the idea of fans. For the first five years of my career I could hardly bring myself to look at the audience. It wasn't about the fans, of course. It was about me, and how I felt about myself. I felt that I hadn't worked hard enough for the cheers and adoration. At the core of this was a lack of belief in my ability and talent, and a sense that I didn't deserve my success.

It was also a shock to go from the bubble of a TV studio to suddenly seeing all of the people who had actually voted for me. It was overwhelming and my instinctive reaction was to hide! It took me quite a while to get my head around it and finally feel comfortable on a stage.

Nowadays, I am so content and proud to be completely who I am as a mainstream pop artist that for as long as the fans – existing or new – buy into it, I will be with them till the end! No more looking over their heads, resenting having to be on a stage because secretly I have no confidence in what I'm doing. No more thinking that what I do is an 'easy sell'. For the last five years whenever I gig I look the people in the eye and I think, I love you for sticking with me, for seeing the real me and being part of it . . .

. . . Now go and buy a Will Young car air-freshener from the merchandise stand, you fuckers!

'You think *you've* had a bad day?'

... I say to the homeless girl.

A crowd has begun to form on the South Bank. It is 6 p.m. on a clear, early spring evening. The sky is a pale pinky haze and the light is reflecting off the Thames. There are children skipping on their way to the theatre with their parents. A lone seagull flaps along contentedly, skimming the water, lazily eyeing up the riverfront for titbits from someone's evening meal on the hoof. A few people are looking out over the river, waiting for partners, loved ones, friends and family. Most, however, have decided to stop and listen to a pop star take on a homeless girl in a new show entitled *Who is Having the Worst Day?*

The stakes are high. Pride was one of them to begin with, but I have certainly thrown that out of the window, along with decorum and grace. We are playing for honour now. Honour and the right to wallow.

Will Young goes first. He has depression, has recently been on an intensive therapy course for eight days in Sussex and still feels a fair bit of anxiety about himself, particularly his inability to form a relationship and his 'constant crying', which has been going on since 4 p.m. this afternoon. This guy's good.

He's also stopped smoking.

'You think *you've* had a bad day?' I repeat, clasping the sweet girl's hands, which are so dirty they belie her assertion that last night was the first time she had ever slept rough. 'I can't seem to stop crying these last twelve hours and now I have to give a speech for children in there.' I point avidly to the Festival Hall. 'In *there*! For *children* – who most likely won't know who I am and will take one look at my blotchy face and start to cry, too. And then the whole of the Royal Festival Hall will be crying. It will spread like wild fire.' My voice is reaching a crescendo. I angle slightly towards my audience. 'I AM GOING TO MAKE ALL THE CHILDREN CRY!'

I gaze around at them on this finishing note, letting it hang in the air and defying them to side with the girl. I might also whisper again, between heavy breaths, 'the . . .' (heavy breath) 'children . . .' (heavy breath) 'cry . . .' It's a sure-fire winner. I mean, I end on my *knees*, for Christ's sake.

The onlookers are impressed, I can see. Some are reaching for cameras, others for their phones – not, I think, to take pictures but to dial 999 and ask the police to come and remove this strange man who has decided to take on a homeless girl and scream, 'I am going to make all the children cry!' on a nice sunny evening on the South Bank. Some, I can tell, are thinking, It's people like him who ruin this country. Drugs do this to a man.

I beg to differ – depression does this to a man. But I have no time to explain all this. I've got a speech to give and an argument to win. This is like one of those freestyle battles rappers do, but for unhappy people. Rather than rhyming over a beat, you proclaim your woes in a public place. To someone who has far more problems than you do.

The girl looks beaten. The match is over. People start to turn away. Then, suddenly, there is a sharp inhalation of breath from the crowd. I look to my right and see my opponent has rallied. She stretches to her full height of five foot two, points at me and says, simply, 'You.'

Then again, still pointing, eyes blazing. 'You.'

She starts low and soft then builds to her own crescendo. 'You ... you ... YOU ... YOOOOOUUUU!' This last one ends with a banshee's wail in one long, guttural, 'oooooooooooooooooohhhhhhh'. It's quite impressive, frankly.

'YOU!' she cries again. '*You* cannot *possibly* have had a worse day than *me*! You are famous. You have money, nice clothes.' She points out my coat to her admiring public, who are warming to her by the second. 'You get driven around, you have food, you probably have friends and you are clean. I slept on the streets last night. I have no money, no food, no shelter, no friends, no boyfriend and no prospects. How can you say YOU are having a bad day?'

She juts out her jaw in defiance, a glint of victory already in her eye. She knows it's a winning performance. Silence fills the air. I look at her. She looks at me. I bow my head. It is patently obvious that this girl, who even with a mucky, tear-stained face is clearly very pretty, has had a far worse day than me. We smile at each other and hug as the crowd disperses. She feels my pain and I hers. Even though we have such different lives and are such different people, in that moment we understand that we are joined in our sadness. *Of course* I have far less to worry about, and she is kind to look for a while past her own problems to see some of mine, so clear in my eyes. We hug again and I give her enough money for a hostel or whatever she chooses to do with it. In return I get ten seconds of kindness and empathy from her and that is more than enough. There I was, going on about the children, and she is barely past childhood herself.

Anyway, the children will not wait and I make to move. The girl turns round before she walks round the corner of the BFI and calls out, 'I like some of your music but not all of it, by the way.'

I shout back at her, 'Come nearer and say that and I'll throw you in the river,' and she disappears around the bend, smiling.

As I set off towards the Festival Hall I hear an old lady mutter to her husband, 'He said he would make the children cry and *then* he said he was going to throw that poor homeless girl into the river. That's the problem with these reality shows.'

I pick up my pace, realising that after my showdown with my new friend the kids might very well be crying anyhow from having to wait for so long. I arrive through the backstage and am shown up to a box. I join a lady councillor who is wearing flares and a bottle-green polo neck under a jacket – an outfit that my grandmother used to wear and which I am coveting quite badly. My grandmother also drove a Triumph Stag and I used one in a video once. My God, I am my grandmother!

With this revelation knocking around in my head, the show starts. It features a charity called igospel.uk, which uses the power of gospel singing to set young people on the right path. It really works – the young people here today are all well behaved, happy and great singers.

Part way through the show, they release their secret weapon. As one song ends, the choir master turns to the audience and says, 'Now it's time to welcome our guest singer to the stage . . . Isaac. Everybody!'

There is a murmur from the four-hundred-strong choir that slowly grows into a chant: 'Isaac . . . *Isaac* . . . ISAAC.' It is just like that bit in *Gladiator* when the crowd calls out for the special . . . gladiator. The children carry on chanting but still no one emerges. The audience is getting restless. Then, from stage left, Isaac appears. He is a young man of about twenty with a large build. He makes his slow dignified way to the centre of the stage. The musicians start up and then . . . Isaac starts to sing. I am halfway through my second pot of ice cream and still eyeing up the councillor's mustard flares when I hear Isaac's voice and promptly throw my ice cream up into the air in shock. The voice is sublime. The ice cream lands at my feet. The voice is actually *unbelievable*. I start to shake with excitement. Wow! This boy sings from his soul. His expression is fairly understated, as are his movements, but out of this big low-key boy comes the most characterful voice I have heard in quite some time.

Isaac has the audience on their feet. I feel like I am in church! He finishes his song and we all applaud wildly. I have also begun to cry again. Fucking hell, Isaac – you've made me cry and it's almost time for my speech. The councillor sees my tears, looks at the ice cream on the floor, and says, with genuine concern, 'It's okay, Will, we can always get you another one.'

The time has come for me to give my speech. I slip from the box to side of stage to wait for my introduction. I have decided – caught up in this new wave of excitement generated by Isaac's performance – to do away with my speech. I am going off piste. I am going to speak from my heart.

This, given historical evidence, is a very, *very* bad idea. Faye is with me and sees me purposefully place the speech down on a chair. Her eyes widen with concern.

'Er, babe, you're not gonna forget your speech, are you?'

'It's okay, Faye.' I raise my hands in a settling, authoritative manner. 'It's okay. I have decided to go off piste.'

Faye turns pale. 'Please don't go off piste,' she whispers.

'I'm going off piste, Faye. This time I can do it. I feel it is right.'

She clutches my arm. 'Please, *please* don't go off piste.'

'I shall speak from my heart, Faye. From my heart – for the children and their parents. I will not make them cry.'

'I'd rather you *did* make them cry than make up your speech. Babe, remember what happens every time you decide to do this. You are *not* Stephen Fry.'

I pause and consider this. Faye is not wrong. There have been several occasions when I've decided, on the spur of the moment, to ad lib rather than read a speech. It has always ended in disaster. One of the first times I did this was at a launch for Women's Aid, a charity that helps women who have suffered from domestic violence. The launch was at the BT Tower. Afterwards Faye said it was better to keep my speeches shorter and not to stray from what was written, as journalists had started to leave when

I began talking about the importance of cordless telephones and my collection of special-edition phone cards.

I also went off piste at an earlier Catch22 event. I was giving a speech to a room full of potential investors and Princess Anne. My job was to woo, flatter and hopefully secure some continued and new support from these various City firms. I started my speech well enough but then again veered off track and ended up saying how capitalism and greed have led to large parts of society becoming disenfranchised, and how it was no wonder our young people are forgotten about. Effectively, I slagged off the business ethos of all the people Catch22 were hoping to gain support from. I then capped this by arguing with Princess Anne. She disagreed with my speech and I disagreed with her, which didn't go down too well with some of the other luminaries. But she was quite cool, actually, and the fact that she was wearing a headscarf and Jackie O sunglasses indoors was enough for me to forgive her for her pro-capitalist leanings.

The list goes on. At a Water Aid charity ball, held to raise money for communities in Africa, I complained on stage about my water rates going up! At a Marks and Spencer event I asked – between *every* song – for a loyalty card that would give me 50 per cent off. They cut my set short. Actually, my onstage banter full stop is famously horrendous. In Ireland, I said that we were all part of the UK, weren't we? I also mentioned the potato famine!

Another infamous blunder took place in Belfast, when I pointed out people in the audience *who weren't there.* My friend Michael Gracey, the tour's art director, was very keen about me saying hello to the audience, particularly those at the back, as they were so far away. He was so adamant about this that he would come up and mime to me while I was singing to say hello to the back. In fact he would often direct me during the shows. I would be singing 'Leave Right Now' or prancing around with the dancers in 'Your Game' and would suddenly see Michael striding up the aisle from the sound booth to stand in the front of the audience, gesturing to me or the dancers to do something. I once asked him not to direct me while I was ad libbing, to which he replied if I ever got it right, he wouldn't have to.

On this particular night in Belfast, Michael was leaving for Australia. He texted me from the airport: 'Say hello to the people at the back. Don't forget. I know you will forget so DON'T FORGET. Don't ad lib too much, either. People want to hear you sing, not hear bad jokes. MG.'

My reply was: 'Dear Michael. I will NOT FORGET. I

will also not miss you directing me through my performances. WY x.'

I did miss him actually, but I didn't forget to wave to the
people at the back. I asked for the lights to come up, with
a smug look in my eyes, thinking, I'll show Michael Gracey
I can remember. But the lights didn't come up. I asked
again, this time with a bit of irritation in my voice. Still no
lights. There was no frigging way I was not going to say
hello to those people at the bloody back after all this, so,
with definite purpose, I turned towards the lighting deck
with a fixed smile on my face but steel in my eyes and
demanded, 'Come on, Simon. Let's get those house lights
up and SEE THE PEOPLE AT THE BACK, HUH?'

Kenny, the stage manager, was gesturing 'no' but there
was no stopping me.

'LIGHTS ON, SIMON!'

The lights finally came on. The back of the stadium was
illuminated in brilliant light to reveal a whole bank of
empty seats.

There was silence. I looked at Kenny, who mouthed, 'I
tried to tell you.'

The lights slowly faded down on the sea of grey plastic
chairs. All eyes were on me. I stood there. What could I
say?

'This next song is called "Evergreen".'

Inside, I wept.

I texted Michael after the show: 'All fine with people at the back. They really appreciated it.'

When I *did* have an audience, I often managed to insult them by accident. Once, at Ronnie Scott's, I made a joke about Labradors and then said I shouldn't as it made me sound even more middle class and therefore segregated me from the audience. Quite what I was saying about them I don't know. I pretended to faint.

In Brighton, someone held up a sign saying, 'WILL, I AM YOUR BIGGEST FAN'. I laughed and said, 'Wouldn't it be funny if that woman really was my *biggest* fan?' Too late, the spotlight revealed a woman who must have been at least twenty-five stone. I pretended to faint.

At Wembley, I filmed the show for a DVD. There was one song called 'Dance the Night Away', which was a bit of a filler. People would often go to the bar during that one. Because the show was being filmed, I was extra nervous and as I got to this song I could see that a row to my right were really not getting involved. Michael had suggested that I should get everyone standing up and dancing to give that part of the show more energy. All of Wembley were getting involved apart from this one row. I was fucked if this was gonna happen. I kept on coming over to the right-hand side of the stage and doing everything I could to get these people to dance, but they just weren't having it. I even shouted, 'Come on, you guys over there. God – some people just don't want to have a good time, do they?'

My friend Adam came backstage afterwards and said, 'Great show, Will. You know, my favourite bit was when you tried to get the disabled row to stand up.'

You can see the moment recorded for posterity on *Will Young Live at Wembley Winter Tour 2004* when I try for a whole song to get a row of some twenty disabled people to stand up out of their chairs.

That was the day, I believe, that I first truly thought I was Jesus.

'Babe, you just shouldn't go off piste tonight. Think of the kids,' Faye persists.

She's right – I have messed up on many occasions by straying off track but I firmly believe that tonight, after everything I've just been through – the crying, the battle with the homeless girl, the crying, Isaac, the ice cream, the crying – I have the right to speak from my heart and go off piste. I look her straight in the eye.

'Faye, this *has* to be done.' I march towards the stage.

Faye lets out a whimper and runs off to hide.

The audience of some three thousand parents and onlookers erupt into excited and welcoming applause as I appear from the wings. I feel strong. I am walking with purpose towards the lectern that has been placed in the centre of the stage in front of four hundred children ranging from five to sixteen years of age. I feel almost presidential. The choir master is standing next to the lectern with my microphone. I calmly take the mike off him, hug him, then whisper in his ear: 'I'm going off piste.'

He looks at me. We have never met before. 'I don't know what that means,' he says.

I nod, as if we have just shared some unspoken understanding, and turn to the audience. There is silence in the room. An expectant silence. I look around, taking in the whole of the Festival Hall, and begin to speak.

But very little comes out. I even struggle to remember the name of the borough that has staged the event and is one of Catch22's biggest supporters. In fact, I can barely remember Catch22's name. My face pours with sweat – it is beginning to drip down onto the lectern. My knees are shaking and the connection between my brain and my mouth seems to have been severed. But then I am thrown a lifeline. One of the children has come up behind me and tugged on my jacket. I turn around and bend down to him, microphone in hand. I ask him what he wants and he looks up at me and says, 'Can I have a hug, please?'

Not only does this melt my heart, it almost brings on my tenth bout of tears of the day. I give him a hug and the audience, who were becoming restless/suspicious, erupt into applause. I stand up and realise I'm on to a winner. Then, just as I'm thinking this, another child asks for a hug. The parents go wild. This is great! What was going badly is now becoming a massive success. I stand up fully, look at all the children and hold out my arms, saying, 'Well, let's all have a group hug, then!' The parents are still clapping

and laughing. I am laughing. The kids are laughing. I even spot Faye appearing from side of stage with a smile and a look of relief and pride on her face.

The kids, however, are getting overexcited. It's like I've given them the order to fall out. They rush from the back of stage, clambering over each other for a hug. The back rows start pushing into the other rows of the choir and suddenly kids are being knocked to the floor. The little ones are getting squashed and some are beginning to cry. The parents slowly stop their applause and the smiles are disappearing from their faces as they see the pandemonium that is breaking out on stage. Microphone stands are falling left, right and centre. Some kids are losing control now, having been so good for so long, and are just jumping up and down with excitement. Others are still moving forward and the whole place has disintegrated into absolute chaos. The choir master stares at me and mouths, simply, 'Why?'

I look out at the parents, all of whom have fallen quiet. And then, to the sounds of crying, screaming, overexcited children and a disappointed choir master struggling to regain control, I turn and walk slowly off the stage. Once again, the off-piste gamble has failed and – as predicted – I have made the children on the Royal Festival Hall stage cry.

'You still doing music, Will?'

I don't know how many jobs there are where complete strangers constantly remind you what it is you actually do, but being a pop star is certainly up there. Most days – most hours, in fact – someone will pass a comment on me or my work.

These comments can come in many guises. There are sweet and encouraging ones:

'Love that song you sang, Will – "Leave Right Now", wasn't it?'

'I voted for you, Will! My partner voted for the guy with the stutter.'

'Loved you on *Fame Academy*, Will.'

. . . To the back-handed compliment:

'Actually, Will, I quite like that song of yours.'

'Well, I went with the missus and you're not really my cup of tea, but the concert was pretty good.'

'I've never really enjoyed what you've done before, but the new song is all right.'

. . . To the questions:

'So, what do you make of that Simon Cowell?'

'Are you watching this year's *X Factor*?'

And then there is my nemesis, the question that sends a shiver down my spine and makes me thank God that I've had therapy:

'You still doing music these days, Will?'

WHAAAT? That is simply the worst question to be asked. It's a bit like going up to a lollipop lady and asking, 'Hello, are you still helping these kids across the road?' Of course, I know there's a difference. You can see the lollipop lady doing her job right there in front of you, whereas if someone hasn't seen me on the TV or heard me on the radio for a while, then how the hell should they know if I'm still doing music? But still . . . it's like a knife to the heart.

It's a very interesting test of ego. Whenever I release a new album, I'll work as hard as I can to get it seen and heard by as many people as possible. After doing countless TV shows and radio interviews – and then even more if the album does well – I kind of egotistically presume that everyone in the country will know: WILL YOUNG HAS A RECORD OUT! This is, of course, not the case.

The really tough thing about that question is how completely demoralising it can be! For example – on the week that *Echoes* goes in at number one, I answer my front door to a young guy selling tea towels. He is really polite and in between showing me his produce his head tilts as he begins to recognise me. Then the inevitable question comes . . . I can tell from the quizzical look in his eyes what he is going to ask, and sure enough, out it comes: 'Are you . . . er, are you still doing music?'

I want to throw his tea towels into the road, drop to my knees and scream: 'Did you not watch *Graham Norton* the other day? *Daybreak*? Who watches these shows? Is there a reason why I got up soooo early? Oh God. OH GOD!'

'Yes,' I reply, quietly.

Another time, I'm buying a phone in Selfridges when the guy serving me asks, 'Do you still do pop music these days?'

I want to cry! I want to walk around with laminated copies of statistics from my latest album stapled to my chest, highlighting that I am still relevant and I do still matter in the pop world and people still *like* me.

'I'VE JUST DONE BLOODY *VOGUE*!' I want to shout out to the other shoppers. 'Four stars in the *Guardian*! DOES THAT MEAN NOTHING TO YOU PEOPLE? THIS IS RELEVANCE – ISN'T IT?' I want to run from floor to floor, throwing my album at people, shouting, 'Listen to it – it's really good.'

I want to race through each department beating my chest like a chorus member from a Greek tragedy. *The Bacchae*

comes to Selfridges – starring Will Young, half naked in Kitchen Appliances, spouting his latest sales statistics.

'It has just gone to number one. Radio 1 won't play it, but they did allow me to come in when it charted and young people listen to Radio 1. I know 'cos Olly Murs was in that day and there were lots of young fans outside. Some of them wanted my autograph (some ignored me). But look . . . look and listen. I am still doing this. I AM STILL DOING THIS!'

I break down on the escalator, megaphone in one hand, new Dries Van Noten cardigan in the other.

Joking aside, for a self-critical perfectionist, comments like these are my deadly enemy and a few years ago would have sent me into a complete tailspin. Nowadays it is par for the course. I recognise that I have a choice to either get wound up or not and I prefer not to be wound up. Life can be tough enough! So I have learned to consciously switch off. But there is still a crazy man inside me who wants to run naked down the Mall crying, 'Have you seen my latest video? It's brilliant and shows I am *very much* still active as a pop star. I mean, I'm dancing with a shopping trolley, for fuck's sake.'

The Mall, by the way, was recently the venue for one of my greatest achievements – I finished my second marathon there. The London Marathon is one of the best things I have ever done in my life – I ran it in 2011 and 2012. The first year I achieved another lifetime ambition, too – meeting Sue Barker. I was also happy to meet Clare Balding. Anyone else I would have been very disappointed with.

I've met a few sporting people over the years. I actually met Sally Gunnell at the Mall as well, when I was singing in front of Buckingham Palace for the 'hand-over concert' to celebrate the coming of the Olympics. I spied Sally Gunnell in the crowd and – as an avid 400-metre runner in my youth – became very excited. Sally, for those of you who might not know, won gold in the 400-metre hurdles at the Barcelona Olympics and is responsible for two of my favourite sporting commentary lines:

'Gunnell goes for gold. Gunnell gets the gold.'

And:

'She looks like she has spurted on the track.'

I saw Sally Gunnell from afar and rushed up to her, tapped her on the shoulder, and all I could say was 'Gunnell goes for gold. Gunnell gets the gold.' Then I walked away. It was very odd.

But the strangest sporting moment of my life took place at another palace – Beckingham Palace. Singing for David

Beckham is another moment I would perhaps like to forget. It was around the time of 'Leave Right Now'. Victoria Beckham had come back to 19 Management by then and had brought David with her. Simon Fuller was beginning to work his magic with the Beckham brand and it was fascinating to watch.

I had met the Beckhams briefly at a celebration of '19 years of 19 Management' (my management company) at the Albert Hall. That was their first public appearance since Rebecca Loos had put her two cents in and David appeared repentant and shaven-headed on the red carpet. There were shit-loads of press. I had just broken up with my boyfriend and decided to walk the red carpet in a stripy jumper and a bowler hat. I too had chosen to shave my hair off that night for the performance. I was trying my best to get close to David, to show I too was going through some personal problems.

It was a great show. Victoria Beckham performed on a throne. I did my first-ever performance with dancers. Cathy Dennis sang Britney Spears' 'Toxic', as she had written it. She went for it as if she actually *was* Britney and I think some people would pay good money to see her performance. I have a copy.

My other special memory of that night was seeing my

mother and godmother at the after-show party sharing a plate of chicken skewers with David. I think my mother was trying to feed him one before I intervened.

'His eyes are too close together,' she said, as I pulled her away. 'But other than that . . . perfect.'

I shared my mother's love of David, so when Victoria rang me up a few weeks later and asked whether I wanted to be the surprise guest/singer at David's birthday party, I leaped at the chance. I can remember exactly where I was when she rang me. I can remember so vividly because I was hanging her husband's calendar on the back of my study door.

The phone rings.

'Hello?' Hammer in hand.

'Hi, Will? It's Victoria. Victoria Beckham.'

Hammer drops.

'Victoria! How lovely to hear from you. I was just . . . er . . . I was just hanging a . . . picture.' I sit down at my desk.

'Would you like to sing at David's birthday? He's a big fan. He's got *Friday's Child* in the car – you and a load of rap!'

'No way?' I reply, distracted. I am flicking through the calendar. *Flick.* June: David in the gym. *Flick.* July: David on the beach. 'That is so brilliant, Victoria. Of course, I would love to sing at his party. I actually have quite a few calendars of David in the house! One for every floor! Ha ha!' I laugh manically.

Victoria laughs, too – a little, worried laugh. 'Imagine that,' she says.

'Imagine.' *Flick*. August – and David's reclining on a sofa.

'O . . . kaaay. Well, we'll see you at the house in a few weeks. And maybe you should fly out with me to see David playing in Spain?'

'Well, that would be amazing!' (September: David's kicking a ball . . . topless, obviously.) 'Thanks, Victoria!'

We say our goodbyes and that is that. I am booked. I AM GOING TO BECKINGHAM PALACE!

Flick. December and we chatter away. Just me . . . and David. 'This time next Christmas I could be buying you that . . . that actually truly horrible jumper, David. This time next Christmas . . .'

The day comes for the party. I arrive and hide in their sitting room. It's a nice house, that's for sure. I hang around, making sure to take a picture of myself in their downstairs loo, and then sneak around behind the marquee. The plan is for me to start singing and then one of the marquee walls will be dragged back to reveal me and the guitarist, Joseph.

It all goes to plan. I start singing 'Light My Fire', then

move on to 'Leave Right Now', another rendition of 'Light My Fire' and then it is over. As I'm singing I notice Catri from the office and her husband George in the crowd. When I catch up with them later, they describe my expression when, after the performance, David bounded up to give me a big kiss and a hug. He had his back to the audience so I was looking out at the whole marquee as he hugged me. Apparently, my face went a deep shade of purple. Of course he was going to give me a kiss hello, I thought afterwards. He is friendly with Elton. He likes gays.

David invites me over to his table and I suggest very quickly that perhaps we could take a stroll around the garden first. The key was to get him out of there. He agrees and off we stroll with Romeo, who was a baby at the time. I try my best to sound nonchalant. I am, of course, a complete, quivering wreck.

By the time we reach the rockery we have touched on the pressures of fame, football, travelling to Spain, I have given all my knowledge on flowers . . . and then David takes a tumble. He goes down, baby and all. I grab on to him as if he is about to be attacked by two Rottweilers.

'It's okay, I've got you,' I shout. 'I've got you, David.'

A security man comes running.

David and the baby are fine.

'Phew, that was close,' says David. 'Thank God—'

'Thank God you're okay,' I interrupt, still holding on tight.

He glances up at me. 'Well, thank God I didn't drop the baby?'

'Huh? Oh, yes! Yes! Of course. The baby. The baby. Yeah, I mean, thank *God*!'

My mind had never stopped to think about the defence-less child in David's arms. Shit. I look at the security man.

'Thank God the baby is all right,' I say, earnestly.

He looks back evenly. He knows exactly what I was thinking. 'Yes . . . sir.'

I never got invited to fly on the plane to watch David play in Madrid.

Batten down the hatches

I have just come back from holiday in Italy. Things didn't go brilliantly.

A bout of melancholy/depression/whatever you want to call it emerged like an angry butterfly from the chrysalis. It takes a lot of thought, energy and time, first to control and understand and then to deal with it. To search my mind and work out where this is coming from. To recognise the triggers and then use the techniques I have built up from years of therapy to ascertain what the fuck is actually going on and then how to box it up. Depression is a beast that shouldn't be fed, but at the same time it is a delicate process because it still needs careful thought and attention.

It has been tough. I don't think anyone really knew what was going on, bar one friend with whom I shared a brief conversation. I would go to dinner each night and get mini-panic attacks about keeping up the appearance. I wanted to run for the hills most evenings. The thing that saddens me the most is hiding this from friends. Sometimes I can share it, but sometimes it just makes the situation worse – and I never want to worry the people who are closest to me. I get concerned about affecting their holiday, their precious week to relax. If I say something then I can feel people looking at me. *Is Will depressed today? How is he doing?* This is a problem for *me*, not my friends. It is one of the things I dislike most about my own depression. I feel like I am letting people down by feeling so low.

To make matters worse, I am like an open book when it comes to my feelings – very easily read. So, if I am feeling bad, I find it extremely hard to cover it up – but cover it up I do. And then I feel as though I'm deceiving the people close to me. The alternative is to tell them what is going on and then feel the burden of being the person who is always a little bit down and really should just pull his finger out and lighten up.

My job can offer an unpleasant contrast to what is going on in my head. *Echoes* has just gone to number one. It's a project I have wanted to do for years and it was a risk. The reaction to the album has been the best in my ten years as a singer. It's still in the top ten a month later, as is the single, 'Jealousy'. It has been a mega-triumph. But to know this is going on makes things worse sometimes. I know all the caveats and conduits of the mind now. But sometimes things just don't feel any better. Sometimes I feel as if I'm going round and round in one enormous circle, with no improvement whatsoever and no sense of control.

These feelings can just jump in from nowhere and that is the scariest thing of all. It starts in the morning. I wake up, there is that wonderful thirty seconds of blissful sleepy peace ... and then it hits me. Where are my thoughts going to take me today? What is my mood like? If I'm in a bad place, the dark thoughts come swinging into view. *Hello, remember us?* Yes. *You are really shit.* Head under pillow. Not today, please. *Knock, knock – us again. Forget the good things, Will. You are incapable of having a*

meaningful, mature, personal relationship with another man.
End of.

Aha, so it's the relationship angle today. Well, you know I'm working on it and trying my best...

Oh shut the fuck up. Loser. It's embarrassing. You look good and have the trappings but really there is no substance, is there? It is all rather tragic. The looks, the house, the car, the career, the money... but no one on your arm. That's pretty sad.

I give in. Pillow comes off. Yes, you are of course correct. It is sad and everyone else sees it, too.

But then, NO. Fuck you. I set off on a run to clear my head. The bad thoughts still knock around my brain, though, and so the conversation continues, on and on.

No wonder people go mad. The energy and persistence you need just to stave off this inner dialogue are extreme and exhausting and leave me completely drained. I do not blame people for turning to other ways of numbing the pain – drink, drugs, sex, shopping, overworking. Sometimes I wish I could turn more to these, at least it is a bit more rock and roll. Could really boost the record around third single time, come to think of it. Valentine's Day, third single release... and Will goes into rehab. Perfect. Some free column inches. I can see it now: 'POSH GAY REALITY SHOW WINNER CRACKS AFTER DECADE OF DEPRESSION'.

GAY POPSTAR (who went to £10k-a-year private school) IN DRUGS SHOCKER.

WILL YOUNG ORGIES ON ALCOHOL AND MARKS AND SPENCER.

This last one I would actually consider.

Luckily I have a strong self-preservation streak that has never allowed me to go to those places (apart from the M&S Food Hall). I am ever thankful for that. Wherever it came from, it rests there deep inside and reminds me daily that if I was to look for instant solace, the fallout would not be pleasant. So: live through it, attempt to understand it and enjoy the good times.

So here I am in Italy, trying to do just that, in a setting of supposed peace and tranquillity. But, just like new year, the time when you are meant to have the most fun is often the time when you end up having the least. What I hate about these periods is not knowing when they are going to strike. Sometimes I can see them coming: after a high I expect a low. I can sense the wind changing and I'm able to prepare for battle. But other times it just fucking sneaks in from left field and I am left winded for days.

Aaaaaaaaaaaggggggggghhhhhhh!

The key, I think, is to remain calm. When a child of a

friend of mine gets angry he calls it 'getting fuzzy-headed'. I like that. When I get fuzzy-headed it can quickly lead to what I call the chain coming off the wheel. Suddenly I am pedalling while not actually going anywhere. Thoughts are reinforced second by second and panic sets in. The trick is to stop it at this stage. Carefully place the chain back on and start pedalling again slowly, perhaps with a gentle push from someone.

When we all got back at Stansted, I was supposed to get a train home with two of our party, but those awful words 'Rail Replacement Service' were chalked up by the platform so we decided to wait for a taxi. Some people recognised me and came up to ask if I'd enjoyed my holiday. I said it had been fine. But what I really wanted to say was 'It was fucking hard work! I struggled to find peace for most of it. Thanks for asking, though.'

Now that kind of answer is obviously not conducive to a light conversation at a taxi rank with a complete stranger. The other danger is that people – no matter how well-meaning – can react over-sympathetically. They watch. They wonder. They ask themselves, 'Where is he at this week on a suicidal scale of one to ten?'

Or maybe they don't. But either way, how can they understand it? The short answer is that a lot of people

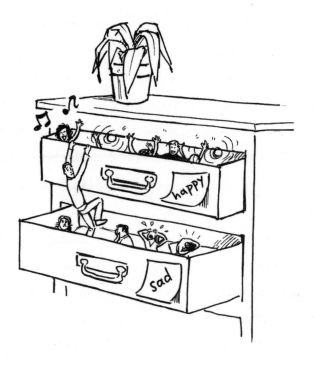

can't and I do not expect them to. It just sometimes hurts me to think that I might be placed in the 'unhappy friend' drawer and, most of all, I don't want to worry my friends.

'She's not very good at fetching, is she?'

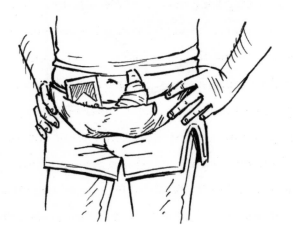

'She's not a retriever, Michael, she's a terrier.'

'Mmm... still. She could fetch stuff, couldn't she?'

'Yeah... I don't actually know if it's their natural instinct to fetch and carry a pack of Marlboro Lights you've dropped out of your pocket. I could be wrong...'

'Oh, I think you are very wrong, William. Very wrong

indeed.' As he says this, Esme trots up, tail wagging, and drops Michael's cigarettes at his feet.

I glare at her. 'Traitor.'

Michael has decided to join me and Esme on our morning walk. He has turned up to the doggy park in full gym gear. From the 1980s. We'd arranged to text when he got there, but I didn't need my phone. Locating Michael was as easy as looking for a nuclear explosion. In effect, he *is* a nuclear explosion . . . of neon Lycra. He has opted for some old Reeboks – inoffensive enough – then some vintage, bright red running shorts (the kind that have slits going right up either side) over a pair of calf-length purple neon leggings. Carrying on upwards there is some sort of complicated layering of tight runner's vestwear and Airtex going on. This is topped off with a bright orange headband and the obligatory RayBans. Oh, and a money belt for his Marlboro Lights. And half a croissant.

'Planning on doing some exercise?' I ask innocently.

'Don't be silly.'

We are sitting on a bench, watching the world go by. It all kicks off in the local park. There is the man who disco dances every morning. He is fabulous to watch. Why run when you can disco dance? (A mantra that many a gay man has followed over the years.) There is the man who exercises by kicking a football against a wall for an hour. There is the all-women exercise group – a tight unit of seven or eight Eastern European athletes. This group is *fierce*. They operate as one, like a version of the tortoise, the old Roman military tactic, where soldiers placed their shields together to form an outer protective shell. That is how these women come across. Impenetrable. I have tried smiles, the odd 'good morning', even once sent Esme in (against her will) to try to forge some sort of bond but to no avail.

The first time I came across the tortoise they emerged round the corner up from the canal and it was all I could do to get out of their way before they trampled me underfoot. Once these ladies start there is no stopping them – momentum and sheer grit carry them forward. They could rival the SAS in their dedication and could probably operate in the same terrifying, deadly manner. Michael and I stay well out of their way.

'Heard from Julia Roberts recently?' asks Michael, once the tortoise has roared past.

'Oh, ha ha, Michael. No I have not "heard from Julia Roberts recently", thank you very much.'

'No, not surprised after your comments.'

Michael gets off the bench, places his left foot next to

where I am sitting and commences the most horrific lunges, so his crotch is basically pumping slowly in my direction.

'Do you have to do that?'

'Two words, loser,' he says, as he continues to lunge towards me. '*Pup Idol.*'

What Michael is so kindly referring to has to be one of my more embarrassing moments with a famous person. It had taken place two weeks earlier in Los Angeles and still the words ring clear in my ears.

I was on holiday in California when a friend suggested that I should sing at the LA Baftas. It was a fairly prestigious gig and I thought it would be a great thing to do, so I agreed. It was being held in some hotel around Beverly Hills. Michael Sheen was hosting. I rehearsed in the afternoon with the pianist – let's call him Greg. He was okay and we did a goodish rehearsal of 'That Ole Devil Called Love'. After that, the plan was for me to go up to the hotel room I had been given as a changing room and get 'freshened up'. There was a period of about four hours between my rehearsal, getting ready, doing the red carpet, sitting down for dinner and then doing the performance.

During the course of these four hours I became more

and more nervous. As I left the dinner table to go backstage to the dressing room, I passed the piano player. Something didn't seem quite right.

'All good, Greg?' I asked.

'Heck yeah. I can't wait to play "Summertime".'

I stopped. Turned to stare at him. 'I'm sorry?'

'"Summertime", man. Yeah, this is going to be awesome.'

'Greg, the song is "Ole Devil".'

'Yeah, man.'

Fuck. He was wasted. Absolutely, undeniably wasted. He was actually hanging on to the table he was standing next to.

I moved up to him very quickly and whispered, 'Greg, have you been drinking?'

'Oh man, just a bit. You know . . . the old Jack Daniel's.'

I was shaking. 'Greg, I am going to say this very slowly and I'm only going to say this once, so make sure you listen.'

He wobbled slightly. 'Okay, man.'

'If you fuck up this performance, I . . . am . . . going . . . to . . . kill . . . you. Do you understand me?'

Greg stopped swaying. 'Oh.'

'Yes, Greg. Oh. Now what I suggest you do is drink

some water. And when I say some, I mean a jugful. Put your head under a cold tap. If you would like some help with this, I would be happy to oblige. Then get a strong black coffee. My friend here is going to watch over you while I get my make-up done. Then we are going to go on stage and you are going to play THAT OLE DEVIL CALLED LOVE really, really well, aren't you?'

'Yes, sir.'

'Yes, sir.' With that, I left.

I went backstage to the small green room, passing Denzel Washington along the way. Ooh, exciting! In the room itself I sat down to have my hair bouffed and there was Paul Bettany, Jennifer Connelly and . . . oh my God – Julia Roberts!

They were all having a very normal conversation about Julia's twins and how she had got her figure back. It was all I could do not to say, 'I'm a twin,' or indeed come in from the other end and say how I had managed to keep my figure after all these years, but I thought, No! Time had taught me that very famous people and me do not mix well.

There are various reasons for this. One is that just because someone is famous, that doesn't *necessarily* make them the nicest person on the planet. Some celebrities get by just by being famous, so they don't need to work on themselves . . . or their behaviour around other people. I don't really see eye to eye with these people, so I have learned not to mix with them. I say this with absolutely no judgement. In fact, I was one of those people for a while and it made me very unpleasant and actually very unhappy. I was convinced that to be famous meant to be cool, aloof and not worry about things like manners and how you treated people. I was too busy and *far* too important to take time with others. The reality was, underneath this 'cool' façade, I was much too busy worrying about what other people were thinking of me and ironically coming across as an arsehole in the process!

One of my favourite tricks of the very famous is that when they become bored with a situation they simply end it by walking away! It's brilliant. They are so used to just moving on from something when it doesn't interest them that they will leave a conversation mid-sentence. Essentially, they don't really listen. I have experienced this a couple of times and I always find it hilarious . . . once I'd got over the shock of someone just wandering off while I was talking to them. Of course, the coolest and normally the most talented stars are nothing like this. They exist peacefully, knowing how good they are at their job, not feeling any need to prove anything. They turn up, do what they need to do, appreciate what they do and appreciate others and they are super-cool human beings.

For years, I was desperate to be a member of the 'famous gang'. Famous people are intoxicating, and they bring a cachet to your life.

'You'll never guess who I saw last night . . .'

'Guess who has just given me his number?'

Due to this desire to fit in and actually just general social awkwardness – I have often said rather strange things around famous people.

When I was performing at the Queen's Golden Jubilee I told Dawn French that I loved her sense of humour. 'In fact,' I confided, 'I base my own humour on *French and Saunders* . . . which is probably why no one laughs at me.' Essentially, I insulted Dawn French when I was trying to pay her a compliment!

Annie Lennox was another example. I am a *huge* fan of Annie Lennox. I bumped into her while I was queuing for my lunch at the Jubilee. It was round the back of Buckingham Palace, which was surreal. Actually, it was a surreal experience full stop. I had recently won *Pop Idol* and now I was performing at the Jubilee with all these music icons. (I even met the Queen.) There was a rule that no one could swear on the microphone during sound check –

a rule broken only by myself and Ozzy Osbourne. The reason was that I had been given an extra performance at the last minute. Queen were doing a medley and Phil Collins suggested that I sing 'We are the Champions'. Sound check did not go well. I remember looking at Tara, who managed Annie Lennox, and asking for her honest opinion. And she said, honestly . . . 'It was terrible!'

As I recuperated at lunch, nestled between Eric Clapton and Mis-teeq, I was enthusing to Annie Lennox's singers about how great they sounded in rehearsal. Suddenly, up she popped behind me.

'Hi, Will. Would you like to join me for lunch in my dressing room?'

I freaked out. She was one of my idols. One of the top voices in pop *ever*! My reply . . . ?

'Er . . . sorry, I can't. I have to go and learn my music.'

I bottled it. I remember sitting by the lake in the gardens afterwards, thinking, Why did I just do that?

I think she realised I was just nervous because she found me later and I did go and chat to her in her dressing room. She was lovely.

This did not stop me years later from putting my foot in it again. I saw her backstage after one of her gigs and asked where she was going off to next.

'America,' she replied.

I had noticed there was a strong anti-war message in her show and so thought my subsequent reply was the correct course to take. 'Huh, America. Well, FUCK America!'

She stopped, looking a bit bemused. 'Er ... yes, well, three of the band members are American.'

I actually wanted to die in that moment.

This leads me back to Julia Roberts. There have of course been other moments over the years – David Beckham, for example – but I feel Julia is the pinnacle.

I sat there in the dressing room being patted down and preened before going on stage to sing my song. All thoughts of drunken Greg had disappeared. It was *all* about Julia. For once I felt I was being reserved. I had already stopped myself from joining in on the pregnancy conversation. I was of course well aware of Julia's children, being a fan. I decided to stay out of it and just observe her in my mirror. It was she who opened up the dialogue.

'Hi, I'm Julia.'

Sorry? She couldn't possibly be talking to me. I carried on minding my own business.

'Er ... hi, I'm Julia,' she repeated. 'And your name is?'

She *was* talking to me. She was talking to me! 'Oh, gosh. Um ... hello! I'm Will. Will Young.'

As I said hello I became aware that the theme tune to *Pretty Woman* had – from nowhere – started playing in my head. Dum dum dum dum dum dah dee dum . . . It started getting louder and louder. Please go away. Not now. Julia Roberts is talking to me.

'Ah yes.' She smiled that famous, million-kilowatt smile. 'You're that guy who won *American Idol*, right?'

'Ah well, yes, in England actually, so it was called *Pop Idol* over there.'

'Right.'

So far, so good.

I could have left it there. I should have left it there. I didn't leave it there.

Overawed by her beauty, and with the theme tune still playing in my head, I piped up, 'Ha! Wouldn't it be funny if it was called *Pup Idol*?'

'I'm sorry?'

'Oh . . . er . . . wouldn't it be funny if it was called *Pup Idol*? Then everyone could bring their puppies.'

Pause.

'You're very beautiful.'

Another pause.

The look Julia Roberts's PA gave me could have turned someone to stone. (I wish it had.) It was a look that said: 'Oh, right, you're one of *those*. You're a psycho fan. I need to get my artist out of this room right now.' Which she promptly did.

I turned back to the mirror.

'You're sweating quite a lot, aren't you?' said the make-up girl.

She dabbed me down and I walked in a daze to the side of stage to be met by Greg, who was still swaying slightly but seemed a bit more compos mentis.

As I stood there, waiting to go on, he sidled up to me and whispered, 'You know, man – I'm not really a jazz pianist. I'm more of a rock guitarist.'

I carried on looking straight forward.

'Great. Just great.'

'Have you declared SORN?'

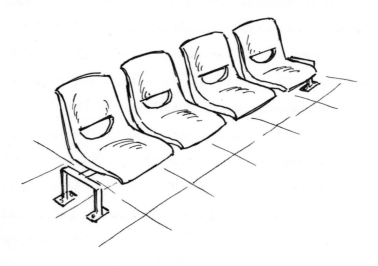

I would challenge anyone who believes they can hang on to their soul and sanity through any circumstances to do the following: lose your driver's licence or have to re-register your licence to your new address, chase up points on your licence or basically have any problem that requires you to:

248

1) Call the DVLA 'help' line and/or
2) Go to your local DVLA office.

For 1 you will find yourself stumbling through a myriad of tunnels, all starting with an option and a number. By the end of the process, you will feel as if you have turned in on yourself thirteen times and are now essentially committing incest . . . with yourself. You will also have forgotten what you rang for and any essential detail of your life that makes it worth living.

Throughout the process you will be confronted with a recorded voice that is the very definition of passive aggressive – even more so than the lady on the sat nav who tells you to make a U turn when you have clearly missed your exit on the motorway. The man with the soft Welsh voice at the DVLA will guide you to the exit with a smile in his voice then kick you up the arse as he slams the door. All done with perfectly good grace. It doesn't matter which way you try to burrow through this maze, this rabbit warren of options and choices and questions, in your hunt to speak with an actual person. In the end, this arsehole, he of the dulcet Welsh tones, will find you and utter the immortal words 'I'm sorry, goodbye' and then throw you out of the frigging door back into the cold and wet, with no more information than you started with – apart from a constant reminder of their website and the fountain of knowledge that can be found there ringing in your ears. The same website where, if you try to enter, you will be confronted with an endless array of forms with more coded titles than you would see in a NASA laboratory. I don't know whether I need a DB76 form or a 5578 Declaration form or if I should be declaring SORN. What the hell is SORN? Is it some sort of standpoint? A political leaning? A constitutional right, like the Fifth Amendment? I declare SORN.

I have tried to sneak to the finish, so I can talk to someone who is alive and not computerised, by listening intently to the options and then taking the one I think will be the quickest. Option 2, 'Please tell us about any emergency medical conditions' seems like a good one to try. This got me a ring tone immediately but then a recorded message told me I should be ringing another number. Then my Welsh friend found me – of course he did. It's like *The Matrix*. I sneak into the system for a moment but of course am quickly detected and then I lose it, continuously pressing numbers until he delivers the knockout blow. 'I'm sorry, goodbye.' And it's over, I'm gone. Out of the game.

The next time I plump for Option 4, something to do with an online driving licence service. It was a toss-up between that and Option 7, which was for people wanting to discuss their personalised number plates. I didn't know that personalised number plates still existed. They were very fashionable in the nineties. I actually quite liked the idea of having one: POP 1DL or simply EVRGRN? Anyway, online services it is. What I never understand is, once you eventually *do* get through to an operator, they *never* ask you about the specific option you've chosen and always appear quite happy to talk about anything. The lady I speak to gives me a lifeline (of sorts). Apparently I need to go down to my local DVLA office to get my new registration document and change of address sorted.

Brilliant. Guaranteed people. No options. Just me, in a queue, waiting to see a real person. So off I trundle . . . into the worst experience of my *life*.

As you walk into Wimbledon DVLA office, a few things will happen. First, time stands still. Second, you feel as though you have stepped into a comedy sketch show from the 1970s. Third, you will be confronted with a sign that says: 'Unfortunately there are no public toilets in this building. The nearest public toilets are in Centre Court shopping centre next to Wimbledon station.'

My therapist would call this 'healthy boundary-making'. The statement is clear and precise. There will be no loos in this building and that is fine. The only problem is, the process that is about to take place involves a lengthy waiting period during which the bowels might begin to rumble – but at least I now know where I can go if I need to relieve myself.

Onward I tread, into the unknown. Brave soldier. I march past the no-toilets sign and take an automatic ticket that darts out from a machine like a snake's tongue. Number 276. This feels like a good number. I look at the board. We are on 243.

'This is okay, William,' I reassure myself. 'These things move very quickly. Ah . . . you see, number 244 has already come up. We will be through this in no time.'

I sit down on a grey plastic seat. It is part of a row secured to a metal pole. Someone walks in, goes straight up to the counter and asks if he can post a letter recorded delivery.

As I chuckle to myself, a man sidles up to me and asks, in a Kenneth Williams-style voice, 'Have you declared SORN?'

He makes it sound naughty.

'I'm sorry, have I . . . *what?*'

'SORN. Have you declared SORN?' His eyebrows are waggling about all over the place, as if he's whispering a secret password. This man is wonderful. He stands right next to me in a grey suit that pinches around his tummy. The trousers are pulled up slightly too high. He is leaning casually into one hip, holding his clipboard in one hand against his waist, so it is almost part of his body. Part of his being. Clipboard and man together in camp symbiosis. His hair is mousy brown and greying at the sides and gelled into a side parting. He wears grey Hush Puppies and black socks, visible due to the high trousers. He flicks his hair and smiles. I like him. I know that he knows that he is in full control of this room, this process, his clipboard, in fact everything to do with the DVLA registering system, he is on top of.

'I'm sorry, I don't know what SORN is.'

The explanation is quick and precise. Said in one breath. 'SORN is when your vehicle is off the public road and therefore does not need to be taxed. You need to "declare SORN"' – said with fingers miming the quotation marks – 'or else you may be liable to a penalty. Have you "declared"' – more mimed quotation marks – 'SORN?'

My mouth is agape. He is like the man who covers all the legal details at the end of those adverts you see mid-afternoon on UK Gold. He is clearly gifted way beyond his knowledge of all things DVLA. All I can do is shake my head, so impressed/terrified am I by this crisp onslaught of DVLA facts.

'Is it on the public roads?' he asks.

I nod. Still mute.

'Right, so is it taxed?'

I nod again.

'Okay, then.' And with that he has gone. Sashaying perfectly on to a Polish couple who have just sat down a few chairs along.

As I am recovering from not declaring and now knowing that I don't *need* to declare SORN (which is a relief), I notice that I am feeling a rumbling. The need to go to the loo has come from nowhere. Really? So quickly? But I am *not* going to that shopping centre just to have '276' called out and start the whole process again. The next number is called out . . . '256'. Oh, yes, we are motoring. No problem.

A lady comes in and asks at the counter if her cat can be seen urgently by the next available vet. She is quietly sent on her way.

The room is really filling up and it's getting noisy now. The digital speaker that calls out the numbers as they appear on the screen has competition. A man in his fifties wearing an anorak and carrying a large number of plastic bags is shouting out numbers, too. Just not the right ones.

'258,' says the robotic voice, gentle and affirming.

'374!' shouts the man. Like this: 'Three... seven... FOURRRRRRRRR!' in a sort of Chewbacca voice. He smiles and looks around as he does it, a fair amount of spittle collecting around the corners of his mouth.

I bet he hasn't declared SORN.

'259.'

'One... hundred... and fifty... THREEEEE!' yells anorak man. Complete with a little shift in his chair and a swing of one of his many plastic bags.

People are beginning to move away. Not my friendly, roaming helper, though. He has now come in on the act. He plants himself firmly by anorak man and as the numbers are called out joins in with a reaffirming voice and firm smile to bring calm and clarity back to the room.

'260,' goes the robot.

'Fifty... siiiiiiiiiiiiiiiiiiiiiiiiiiix,' goes mad man.

'Two hundred and sixty,' corrects our roaming helper with an even more assured lean into his hip and clasp of the clipboard. As if that were at all possible.

'261.'

'Five hundred and seventy-eight-tat-tat-tat-tat...'
Shuffle and swing of the bag.

'Two hundred and sixty-one. Nothing to worry about
here, folks.'

I am laughing so much I am starting to weep and this is
not helping my loo situation. It's like witnessing the weird-
est, most bizarre game of bingo I have ever seen. Roaming
helper has started to throw in reassuring phrases at the end
of the numbers. I cannot imagine where this is going to end.

'262.'

'TWO! On its own. THE NUMBER TWO!'

'Two hundred and sixty-two, people – and all's going
well.'

'263.'

'FIFTY-FIVE THOUSAND!'

'Two hundred and sixty-three and patience is the virtue
of us all.'

Genius.

End it does, though. For the next number is crazy man's
number.

'264.'

The man looks up. Looks at his number. Looks up again.
The whole room is waiting with bated breath. Roaming
helper repositions himself, widening his legs but still with

a definite lean into one hip, clipboard ready like the weapon of a Japanese warrior. Mad man is silent. His mouth opens and closes a few times like a goldfish, and then he simply gathers up his bags and moves perfectly normally to the free kiosk.

The whole room breathes again. Our man in grey flannel gives a satisfied sigh, readjusts his hair and calls out confidently: 'Now, anyone importing a car from Germany that hasn't been given a British MOT? And we are talking within the last three years here, ladies and gentlemen...' He moves effortlessly to another part of the room.

I am seriously considering calling him back and telling him to move into politics, but D-Day is approaching. The loo in the Centre Court shopping centre is also becoming ever more appealing, but I'm sure I can make it through this. My forms are filled in. I am primed like a cat, ready to spring with all the appropriate insurance documents, headed letters, bank details, passport, blood type, medical records, GCSE certificates, the lot. I *refuse* to be caught on the hop.

My number is called. '276.' I hear it, I walk up.

Roaming man blocks my path. 'Are you looking to take a car over to Eastern Asia in the next five years, sir?'

I bat him away. 'Not now. I'm here to re-register,' I say firmly. He can see that I mean business.

So does my opponent at the desk.

Five minutes later I am standing in Ryman's, next to Wimbledon station. My forms were filled in with the wrong ink and my insurance *document* was not the correct one so I now have to wait in Ryman's to get the right documents faxed through. You cannot use the fax machine at the DVLA office but Ryman's will offer you their services for a price. They are doing a roaring trade.

It is raining.

'Your papers have come through,' says the spotty youth behind the counter.

I look at him. 'Thank you,' I say, with no feeling at all. He knows what has happened. He's seen it before. So many people go in strong to that building across the road from his shop only to walk out again with a piece of their soul gone. And maybe having wet their trousers.

As I pay for my faxed documents and a biro with a fluffy bird on the end that was an additional purchase to try and cheer myself up, I know what is in store for me. I know I have to go back in there. I know I have to take another ticket, I know that roaming man will come up to me and ask if I have 'declared SORN', and I know that I don't really remember who I am and what my purpose is in life. And I can't remember what SORN is, either.

I put the documents and the pen in the Ryman's bag, turn to walk out the door, and while I look at the entrance to the DVLA across the street, I think of all those numbers and all those forms and a small, desperate little tear rolls out of my eye and down my cheek.

I have been broken.

I've lost my voice

My phone beeps.

It's a text from Michael.

'Come to the café. NOW.'

Then another...

'Waiter here and he's wearing shorts. OMG. SHORT shorts. I am SOOOOO in love.'

'PS bring Esme, it'll be a talking point.'

'PPS dress down.'

This is not unusual, such high drama mixed with

dictatorial demands. The week before I received a text simply saying, 'Help. Urgent.' It turned out Michael was in Liberty's and wasn't sure which Demeulemeester shirt to go for.

It is mid-morning and I haven't been doing much, so I put Esme on a lead and off we trot. The night before had been interesting. When I say interesting, I mean horrific. In fact, yesterday was one of the worst days – work wise – for quite a considerable time. I need cheering up, and when I'm with Michael I'm so busy boggling at his diva demands, bad behaviour and colour-clash outfits that I don't have time to think about my own problems.

The truth is I've been feeling pretty low for some time, but I couldn't put my finger on why. It's just been knocking around, and trying to puzzle it out has been exhausting and unrewarding. Is it:

a. The weather – winter is dark and miserable
b. Loneliness
c. Post-tour blues
d. Out and out depression
e. Any or all of the above
f. Oh fuck it . . .

Last night I read at a carol concert for Mencap, a charity I have supported for ten years. My friend Sarah came with me. I can always trust Sarah to speak her mind. Last spring we'd sat by the edge of the canal in Amsterdam, talking about *American Idol*. I had been asked to perform on the final show that summer.

We were perhaps a little the worse for wear.

'How many viewers is it?' she asked.

'God, about twenty-five million at least,' I replied, staring out over the canal and imagining I could actually grow gills and swim like a porpoise.

There was a pause.

'You'd better not fuck it up,' Sarah said and then, 'I wonder if I ever really could be Supergirl.'

Two months later, I was walking to the stage to sing live at *American Idol*, when my phone beeped just as I was handing it over to Faye. It was Sarah. I read the text.

'Hi. Remember... DON'T fuck it up. Love Sarah x.'

It is thanks to supportive friends like Sarah that my feet have remained firmly on the ground.

The carol concert was moving, and Sarah and I sang along heartily to 'Silent Night'. While I was giving the reading I missed a call from my manager, Terri. I texted her as I left the church to say I would call her back when I got home, but I had a funny feeling that something was wrong.

For the last four months or so, I had been in discussions about becoming a mentor on a show called *The Voice* – a new talent show that had recently been a big hit in America. The emphasis seemed to be placed more on the singer than on the people judging and also the judges couldn't see the auditionees when they first performed, so purely 'the voice' was critiqued.

I watched the reels from America and liked the show and thought that I could do it – I had mentored young singers before and enjoyed it. I thought I could bring a lot to the table, and being involved in a prime-time TV show would boost my profile and help my record. It was a win–win, really. After ten years as a singer and performer, I felt I was experienced enough not to make a fool of myself, so I wouldn't be damaged by the show. At the same time I could help some younger singers, which would be very fulfilling. It could also help my record to reach even more people – a real bonus as I really passionately believed in it.

The process went on and on, with lots of meetings and conversations. I had to remind myself on several occasions not to get overexcited, because jobs that look like they might happen often fall through in the end. In the past, I have missed out on Burberry campaigns, Coke commercials, film parts – the list goes on. If there was one thing I thought I had learned it was to 'chill my boots' until I know for certain that something is going to happen.

Anyhow, the discussions continued. I came down to London while on tour to meet with people and then finally I got the call. I was doing a show for Radio 2 when Terri phoned.

'The production company have just rung. You've got it.'

'I don't believe you.'

'Well, believe me. You've got it. You are going to be one of the mentors on *The Voice*.'

'Are you sure?'

'Yes!'

But even then something sat uncomfortably with me. The fact the call had come from the production company – not the BBC – made me feel uneasy. I always felt – coming from an ITV show – that I was never seen as so much of a 'BBC person'. So I still couldn't really believe it. Slowly, though, it started to sink in – and before long I was over the moon!

I felt that things had really come together this year. I'd made a record I was proud of. I felt I had got back my creative integrity and, even more, my creative confidence. And now getting *The Voice* felt like a huge bonus. The extra thing that I'd been hoping for – the big pay-off for sticking to my guns and fighting my corner and following my heart.

Of course, the real pay-off was the album doing well and still having such a great job after ten years. But at the time I didn't see that and I really yearned for something big. I guess I missed the years of being more famous in some ways. This is me being completely honest now. My sales had dropped and I suppose some part of me still missed selling a million albums, being papped (a very small part of me!), being a bigger star. I guess a part of me slightly lived for that.

It's funny, all of that attention never really sat well with me . . . and yet there is another side of me that misses it when it's not there. Not getting asked to the right parties. Not always getting the biggest gigs. I want to be selling the most, more than ANYONE ELSE! I want to be making more money – MORE THAN ANYONE ELSE! And being the most FAMOUS PERSON EVER! It is Veruca Salt syndrome – the spoilt child who always wants more. The truth is that now I do stuff that I love, that I really believe in, that I think has integrity – and if it all ended tomorrow I could still say I was über proud of my work. The key is to be happy with something before it even leaves the studio and then the rest is a bonus. That is the way I see it now.

The problem with *The Voice* is that I got completely carried away. When I got the gig, my brain went into overload, planning suit ranges, which parties I could go to with such grand exposure, should I do an 'At Home with Will' photoshoot for *World of Interiors* or *Harper's*. Security – will this be necessary? I would imagine so, given my soon-to-be-higher profile. I was one Google search away from private jets. I have a friend who calls this level of delusion the 'Oscar acceptance speech moment'. It's when your brain gets completely carried away and you start predicting what you will say in your acceptance speech before the song or film has even been finished. Well, I was not only writing my speech – I was translating it into Urdu, that's how global I was going, baby!

Despite my foreboding after the carol concert, by the time Terri rang again I was busily writing this script in my head. But as soon as I heard the tone of her voice I knew what had happened.

'I don't quite believe I'm about to say this, Will,' she said. 'But they've retracted their offer.'

Silence.

'Will, did you hear me? They've retracted the offer. They feel the panel needs more balance. They're asking the guy out of The Script to represent "rock". Pretty mind-blowing. They're hardly Led Zeppelin, for f***'s sake.'

Silence.

'Will? Are you there?'

I found my voice. 'Oh, Terri, that is a shame. I did feel perhaps something wasn't quite right. Oh well. You win some, you lose some.'

'You are taking this remarkably calmly, Will. Are you okay?'

'Yes, Terri, I am. It's a shame but, you know, everything is still going great so we've just got to get on with it, haven't we? I mean, they gave me the job and now they have taken it away – but they can do what they like and it isn't going to change it, so that's that.'

'That's a great attitude, Will. But if you want me to come over, I will.'

'No, it's fine – thanks, Terri. I think I'm going to go now as I've got to walk Esme. Let's speak tomorrow.'

'Okay . . . er . . . well done for taking it so well. Call any time.'

'Okay . . . thanks, Terri. Bye.'

I hung up the phone. Calmly placed it down. Stood up from my dining-room table and broke down.

It was quite a thing actually. The straw that broke the depressed camel's back. Everything just seemed fruitless. What the hell was the point? I might as well give up. All my fight had gone in an instant. As I let out reels and reels of sobs, Esme – who I had only had for two weeks – sat in front of me and proceeded to curl out an enormous turd onto the new carpet. As I lay on the floor (by this stage), I looked at her and sobbed, 'And how, exactly, do you think I'm going to be able to afford the dry cleaning for that now?'

I was aware that a touch of dramatic licence was being used here. As was Esme, who promptly left to go upstairs.

I was absolutely gutted. Apart from all the overexcitement, Oscar acceptance speeches, private jets, etc., I had genuinely been looking forward to the challenge. I don't think in ten years I have ever been treated like that, been led on so long for a job, got it and then had it taken away – or ever been so weirdly upset about it. It was a great lesson. A great reminder that this business is a very cruel one indeed.

I had a friend who was dropped by her record company via email. Imagine that:

To: So and so
Subject: You're dropped

Sorry!
Best wishes,
Your old record company

Another friend took a meeting with her music publishers and had to remind them that they actually did already publish her, they just hadn't returned her calls in the last six months!

It is a bloody cruel business and TV is the cruellest of them all. I should have remembered that, having come from TV in the first place. I wasn't prepared for the let-down ... and when you're not prepared, things really can affect you. But as I say, it was a good lesson. A lesson that I should never put my belief in external things; things beyond my control. It should always come from within – and this goes for life in general. External factors change daily, and *The Voice* was a stark reminder of that.

Whenever I hear the show mentioned now I can't help but remember Esme curling out that poo and it seems to raise a chuckle, but at the time the rejection really winded me and took me down even further when I was pretty miserable already. Still, at least I could insert in my list of reasons I might be depressed:

g. *The Voice* ... and a poo stain on my new carpet.

Welcome to Hackney

'Thank you!' I shout back to the sweet lady who has just welcomed me to Hackney. I am moving the rest of my stuff into the house. The sun is shining. I have just driven past a massive billboard on Old Street with my face on it. What a way to enter a neighbourhood. Some people drop round to see the neighbours, others bake a cake, I erect an enormous billboard of my face.

I have been nomadic for a year, since selling my house in Holland Park. I lived in Soho, then Battersea, and I even had a stint in a hotel, where I imagined on a daily basis that I was Noël Coward. Now here I am turning into my square, about to open my front door and walk into my shiny new house. My new album is out, my single is at number five. I have a television special airing tonight and everything is good in the world. Work is good, I am looking good, people are welcoming me to the neighbourhood, I feel popular. In I turn and...

Oh, God. Wait.

There is a pigeon in the road, just outside the school. It is half dead, and being attacked by an enormous crow that is lancing it over and over with its sharp beak. Oh, this is awful. Poor, poor pigeon. I mean, I'm not an enormous fan of London's pigeons, but this is no way to die. I stop the car in the middle of the road and shoo away the crow, which flies up onto the nearest roof.

'You bad, bad bird,' I shout, as if he is going to understand.

The pigeon is flapping its wings half-heartedly. I know

that I will have to kill it. I leave the car and quickly walk round the corner to my house, where I know there are some loose bricks. This will not be pretty. I grab a brick and dash back round the corner to the pigeon ... to find the crow delivering the finishing blow.

'NOOOO!' I shout at the crow as it flies off. 'You horrible, HORRIBLE fucking bird!' I look down at the pigeon. Its eyes are almost closed now. Oh, God. I know what I have to do. I bring the brick down quickly on its head and it is put out of its misery. It is sad and I am panting a little.

Then I hear a small voice pipe up behind me: 'Miss! Will Young has just killed that pigeon.'

I slowly turn around to see a crocodile of stunned schoolkids, around seven years old, mouths agape, staring at me. My gaze scans along the line and finally reaches the teacher. She is looking at me in horrified disbelief. 'Come along, children.' Still watching me warily, she slowly but surely guides the kids towards the school gates. 'Don't look at him, children,' she mutters. 'Don't look at him.'

I stare up at the crow. It gives a loud, satisfied squawk.

'Oh, screw you,' I say and get back in the car.

This is what the children saw:

A man is standing in front of a big, black Jeep that he has parked in the middle of the road. There is a bird in front of the car. He shouts, 'You bad, bad bird.' Then he runs round the corner. Twenty seconds later he reappears with a brick. He shouts, 'NOOOOOO! You horrible, HORRIBLE fucking bird,' and then proceeds to smack the bird on the head with the brick.

This was my entrance to the neighbourhood.

Being smacked on the head with a brick is actually how I have felt these last six months. I have had the longest and hardest period of depression in thirty-three years. Often I have not left the house. I have cried pretty much continually for the last three months. It reminds me of when Michael Jackson died and Madonna tweeted, 'I am crying constantly'. Me and a friend would joke, I wonder if Madonna is really crying *constantly*. Well, now I take that back. I have begun to recognise my feelings of complete self-loathing and confront them. It has not been an easy battle.

I moved into my new home on the night that *Echoes* got to number one. It should have felt like an amazing victory. The record company had told me 'Jealousy' wasn't right, and that the album wasn't finished. (I was played songs by Pitbull and informed that '*This* is the kind of stuff that is selling.' Then they asked if I would maybe consider doing a cover song. Oh, and did I really need to do a video? This was a low point.) After all these battles I should have felt completely vindicated *and* happy. Instead, I felt... nothing. Well, actually, I felt sad and I felt incredibly alone. My default setting, I have now learned. I called Jim and Mima, from Kish Mauve, with whom I'd written most of the record. They were in France, drinking champagne with friends in the sun. I was at home, on my own, feeling very sad.

'Are you really proud?' Mima asked.

'Yes,' I lied. The truth was, I felt no sense of achievement. I just felt shit. After quite a few years of therapy, I still felt shit. It was incredibly demoralising.

Slowly, I have begun to realise that if something starts from any place other than a place of self-love, it will always end up back at that same place again. So if I do something to make myself feel better, make myself feel like I am not a crap person, I will always end up feeling like a crap person. This can be anything: shopping, work, sex, porn, eating, exercise... Such has been the cycle of my life. I won two Brits – I felt I didn't deserve them. I got on radio A-lists – I immediately wanted something else. I got on *Parky* – I felt I did a shit job. The list goes on and on. I got a new boyfriend – I picked holes in him and then in myself for doing so ... ferociously. I've bought houses, done them up, and then, as soon as I've moved in, decided they're not right. I've gone on shopping binges and have never worn the clothes. I've bought old cars and then spent all my time worrying if other people like them. Behind all this is a sense of not feeling good or valuable or lovable. If I don't feel that, nothing will ever be good enough and I will always arrive back at square one.

Things are beginning to change, though. I think I'm at a crossroads. My album deal is up and as I write I'm in the process of signing to Island Records. I'm more excited about my music than ever. I am about to embark on *Cabaret*, the musical. I have never sung, danced and acted all in one place. It is, in a way, one of the final hurdles to jump. I am aiming for brilliance. It is terrifying. It is thrilling.

This book has been exciting, sad, hysterical, emotional, self-informing and a whole lot more. I have written from the heart, and with a mind to giving a true account of what it is like to do my job, to be the person I am, to live with depression, to live with humour, and to see life in a way that works for me and gives me hope for the future. To notice the important things in life and fight to be the most content and grateful person I can be. I have been candid because I have found other people's candour informative and valuable. I hope you might find the same.